To the memory of my parents,

Minnie Coopersmith Gutwill

and

Nathan Gutwill

CONTENTS

PREFACE TO THE FOURTH EDITION

A reference guide that teaches, *Problems in Literary Research* is designed to introduce students of literature, particularly beginning graduate students, to some of the most useful library resources and to bring to the librarian's attention those resources most valuable to the literary researcher. Emphasis is upon English and American literature, though chapter 6 features a section on comparative and world literature.

Though no one would question the necessity for being acquainted with the library's basic reference holdings, nevertheless, students drawn to literature con amore are often dismayed by the extent and detail of the material they must master. I have sought to make the introduction to literary research less formidable by selecting works that are fundamental, either in themselves or as representatives of a class of reference tools. These works constitute the thirty-six main entries (the "M" entries), sufficient to survey the field but not, I hope, to boggle the mind. I have outlined key features of contents and arrangement in order to expedite gaining familiarity with these works.

The review questions are intended to reinforce absorption of the information provided by the outlines. Some of these questions test whether you have retained what you just read in the outlines. (What off-literary subjects are covered? Until what year does coverage extend? How does a keyword index work?) Other review questions test your ability to *apply* the outline information. (Would you expect to find an entry for *Beowulf*? For Mary Wollstonecraft? For Adrienne Rich?) If you are uncertain about your answers, try re-reading the outlines until you have a clear sense of the scope and ordering of the reference work.

The research problems that follow can be solved through the exclusive use of the work just introduced. Solving these problems will give you an indispensable "hands-on" experience under controlled conditions, thus providing the security of knowing that you must master only one reference work at a time and that there *is* a correct answer. Unfortunately, straightforward, supportive pedagogical situations do not always correspond to reality; your future scholarly research projects may be complex and open-ended, but you will cope with ambiguity the better for having confidence in your knowledge of basic reference tools.

Like the research problems, each of the general review problems can be solved by employing one of the works introduced up to that point; here, too, each problem requires the use of only a single reference work. However, in the case of a few dual entries (for example, *Dissertation Abstracts International, Comparative Dissertation Index*), a single problem may call for both works. The general review problems test your knowledge of *which* reference work is likely to yield the solution as well as your skill in using that work. Even if you lack the time to research the answers, the general review questions can help you determine whether you have retained a sense of the kind of information the works introduced contain. For each problem, you need only ask yourself, in which reference work am I likely to find the answer to all the parts of this question?

Under Supplementary Works (the "S" entries), I have briefly described alternative and additional reference tools. Entries 1 through 76 are ordered under subject headings corresponding to those of chapters 2 through 5, within the subheading alphabetically by author or title. Entries 77 through 182 describe reference works in areas becoming increasingly important within English studies—children's literature, comparative and world literature, film, literary theory, and rhetoric and writing studies. In the headnotes and footnotes to the "M" entries, I have supplied bibliographic data only for works not given "S" entries; the scope of these works can generally be inferred from their titles and subtitles.

Like most reference guides, *Problems in Literary Research* is necessarily selective and sometimes arbitrary in its classifications. I have used my own judgment in classifying works that overlap two categories or that are best studied together with a companion tool (a variorum edition and a concordance). I have omitted some excellent alternative works only because they are not significantly different from the main or supplementary entries. You will easily discover these alternatives by yourself because similar reference works are most often shelved beside one another. Although I note the availability of some titles on-line or on CD-ROM, given the constantly changing nature of the market for automated retrieval of information, I have not attempted a comprehensive survey of what is or isn't available. You can keep up with that market through the *Gale Directory of Databases and CD-ROM* (Detroit: Gale Research, 1993-), 2 vols., an annual alphabetically arranged title with a subject index. Because libraries differ greatly in the kinds of computerized information services they offer, I describe print sources even if they are also available on-line. Moreover, the increasing computerization of reference sources (e.g., *Dissertation Abstracts*, *ERIC*, the *MLA Bibliography*) brings with it not only convenience but potential disadvantages. For those unfamiliar with the use of reference volumes, when the computers crash, all research stops. Further, the technologically dependent, like specialized physicians who rely on the latest high-tech equipment, are apt to feel ill-trained for work in modestly furnished facilities. Finally, much useful material is lost when reference works are computerized: I refer not only to data that doesn't "translate" into the software's categories but to introductions recounting the need for the particular tool; its idiosyncracies; and the history of its development, from which we may sometimes infer the development of a discipline. In such elements as these, in the delight of discovery while window-shopping the shelves, lies the human appeal of library research.

Two caveats are appropriate here. First, you should avail yourself of the most recent edition of any reference work as well as its current supplements. When using these works in the course of your professional career, you should be alert to updatings. With a few notable exceptions (*Britannica* and, for some areas, *The Cambridge Bibliography of English Literature*), the most recent edition is the only one suitable for scholarly research. Second, insofar as reference tools are secondary sources, many of the works entered are not suitable for quoting in scholarly papers. In doubtful cases, follow the practice of established scholars.

In preparing this fourth revised edition, I found James L. Harner's *Literary Research Guide*, 2nd ed. (New York: MLA, 1993), especially useful. Other important references guides are James K. Bracken's *Reference Works in British and American Literature* (S2), and Michael

J. Marcuse's *A Reference Guide for English Studies* (Berkeley: University of California Press, 1990). I recommend these to graduates of *Problems*. Also, the exercises at the back of Richard D. Altick and John J. Fenstermaker's *The Art of Literary Research*, 4th ed. (New York: Norton, 1993), offer challenging reference searches on which you can try your wings.

I am indebted to many members of the staff of San Diego State University's Love Library, in particular to Carolyn Fields, Humanities Reference Librarian. My thanks are due to Rachel Litonjua-Witt and James Woods of SDSU's Instructional Media Services, who have put their infinite computer skills at my disposal. I am also grateful to my colleagues Lois Kuznets, Emily Hicks, and Sherry Little, who suggested titles for the Children's Literature, Literary Theory, and Rhetoric sections respectively. My former research assistant Janice Chernekoff helped with the initial development of the Rhetoric section. Above all, I must thank my most recent research assistant, Andrew Beck, for his exceptional diligence and professionalism throughout this project.

And in such indexes, although small pricks
To their subsequent volumes, there is seen
The baby figure of the giant mass
Of things to come at large.

Shakespeare, *Troilus and Cressida*, 1.2.343-46

CHAPTER 1

A BASIC CORE

M1. *The Oxford Companion to English Literature*

M2. *The Oxford Companion to American Literature*

M3. *A Literary History of England*

M4. *Columbia Literary History of the United States*

M5. *The New Cambridge Bibliography of English Literature*

M6. *Literary History of the United States: Bibliography*

M7. *MLA International Bibliography*

M8. *The Oxford English Dictionary*

These are the most basic of reference tools: a handbook, a literary history, and a bibliography for English and for American literature; an international bibliography for updating bibliographies awaiting supplements or new editions; and a (one should say "the") historical dictionary. Together these tools constitute a survival kit for students of literature.

M1. *The Oxford Companion to English Literature.* Ed. Margaret Drabble. Rev. ed. Oxford: Oxford University Press, 1995.

The *OCEL,* a capsule-information handbook, belongs to the useful Oxford Companion Series, many of whose titles have bearing on the study of literature. The *OCEL* is more comprehensive than its title suggests, insofar as it includes a number of non-English authors important in the context of English literature. Oxford Companion (or Dictionary) titles include *The Oxford Companion to Twentieth-Century Poetry in English,* ed. Ian Hamilton (New York: OUP, 1994); *The Oxford Companion to American Literature* (M2); *The Concise Oxford Dictionary of French Literature,* ed. Joyce M. Reid (Oxford: OUP, 1985); *The Oxford Companion to Canadian Literature,* ed. William Toye (Toronto: OUP, 1983); and *The Oxford Companion to German Literature,* 2nd ed., ed. Henry Garland and Mary Garland (New York: OUP, 1986). Related literary titles include *The Oxford Companion to Children's Literature* (S79) and *The Oxford Companion to the Theatre* (S106). Also useful are *The Oxford Companion to the English Language,* ed. Tom McArthur (Oxford; New York: OUP, 1992); *The Oxford Companion to the Bible,* ed. Bruce Metzger and Michael D. Coogan (New York: OUP, 1993); *The Oxford Companion to American History,* ed. Thomas H. Johnson (New York: OUP, 1966); *The Oxford Companion to Art,* ed. Harold Osborne (Oxford: Clarendon, 1970); and *The New Oxford Companion to Music,* ed. Denis Arnold, 2 vols. (Oxford: OUP, 1983). See *Books in Print* (M29) for other titles.

Though a particular Companion may not be the ultimate dictionary-guide in its field, nevertheless, these Oxford titles are worth keeping in mind as reputable factfinders for basic literary and literature-related research.

Contents:

1. Authors, including "historians, critics, philosophers, scholars, and editors" (vi); mostly English but some American, Commonwealth, and European:[1] biographies and works with their dates;[2] occasionally, bibliographic references to secondary works.
2. Works: their nature, and, if a major work, a plot summary.
3. Characters (fictional and historical); under surname unless an indissoluble whole (Peter Pan).

4. Literary groups, movements, publications, prizes.
5. Literary terms.[3]
6. British and Irish mythology.
7. Appendices, pp. 1111-71:[4]
   a. Appendix 1: a chronological outline of British literary works juxtaposed against a list of continental events, literary and political.
   b. Appendix 2: Poets Laureate.
   c. Appendix 3: Literary Awards.

Arrangement:

1. Abbreviations and conventions observed (typography, order of entries, spelling) at front preceding the dictionary proper.
2. Alphabetical: no table of contents or index.
3. Cross-references indicated by asterisks.
4. Appendices at back.

Review Questions:

1. For which of the following would you expect to find entries: Edgar Allan Poe, Mr. Micawber, Neoplatonism, Salomé, sonnet, Cuchulain, Winston Churchill, Søren Kierkegaard, Robin Hood, Honoré de Balzac, Zeus, the Romantic movement, the Globe Theatre, Henry VIII, chapbook, Scottish Chaucerians, oxymoron, Gloriana, Thor, Squire Western, Margaret Atwood?
2. For which of the following would you expect to find plot summaries: Mary Shelley's *Frankenstein, Beowulf*, Pope's *The Rape of the Lock*, Shakespeare's *Hamlet*, Antonia Fraser's *Mary Queen of Scots* (biography), Golding's *Lord of the Flies*?

Research Problems:

1. Define and illustrate an anacrusis. Describe the two principal rhyme schemes of the sonnet. Describe the rhyme scheme and meter of the Spenserian stanza, and name four English poets who used this stanza form.
2. What are Theophrastian "characters"? In which century did this form enjoy a vogue in England? Which English character writer was murdered in the Tower of London?

3. What is Terry Eagleton's critical orientation? With whom did he study?
4. What is the form of *Hudibras*? What occurs in Part I? Name a short satirical poem by the author of *Hudibras*. Who gave him a pension?
5. In what literary work does Gerald Scales appear? Zenocrate? How do they figure in their respective works?
6. Identify briefly: Jean de La Fontaine, Cesare Pavese, Petrus Ramus, Cristoph Martin Wieland.

Notes (*OCEL*)

1. For further coverage of recent English authors, see Part II of *Twentieth-Century British Literature* (S7); *A Guide to Twentieth Century Literature in English* (S103); and *Poetry Today: A Critical Guide to British Poetry 1960-1992*, ed. Anthony Thwaite (London: Longman, 1996). Other alternatives to the *OCEL* are the *Bloomsbury Guide to English Literature* (S9); and the *Cambridge Guide to Literature in English*, ed. Ian Ousley, new ed. (Cambridge: CUP, 1993), especially valuable for its wide international range. Also see Joanne Shattock, *The Oxford Guide to British Women Writers* (Oxford: OUP, 1994); *The Reader's Encyclopedia of Shakespeare* (S3); and the *Dictionary of Irish Literature*, ed. Robert Hogan (Westport, CT.: Greenwood, 1979).
2. For fuller information about standard editions of literary works, see Bateson and Meserole's *A Guide to English and American Literature* (S1), published in 1976, but not yet superceded. A book-length chronological index of works is provided by Martin Gray, *A Chronology of English Literature* (Harlow, Essex: Longman; Beirut: York, 1989).
3. For allusions, now largely excluded from the *OCEL*, check *Brewer's Dictionary of Phrase and Fable* (S12), *The Oxford Dictionary of English Proverbs* (S17), a classical handbook or dictionary (M11, S99), and *The Interpreter's Dictionary of the Bible* (S11). Also useful are *Mythology of All Races* (S71), *Funk & Wagnalls Standard Dictionary of Folklore, Mythology and Legend* (S13), *Britannica* (M36), and specialized historical and biographical dictionaries such as *The Cambridge Historical*

Encyclopedia of Great Britain and Ireland, ed. Christopher Haigh (Cambridge: CUP, 1985), *Steinberg's Dictionary of British History* (S22), *An Encyclopedia of World History* (S72), *The Dictionary of National Biography* (M14), and *Who's Who* (M15).

For literary terms, also see Holman and Harmon's *A Handbook to Literature* (M9), Shipley's *Dictionary of World Literary Terms* (S113), Makaryk's *Encyclopedia of Contemporary Literary Theory* (M10), Richard A. Lanham, *A Handlist of Rhetorical Terms*, 2nd ed. (Berkeley: U of California P, 1991), and *The New Princeton Encyclopedia of Poetry and Poetics* (S6).

4. For other useful appendices, see those in the 5th edition, pp. 1101-05:
   a. "Censorship and the Law of the Press": an essay on the censorship of literature, journalism, and theatrical performances from the sixteenth century through modern times.
   b. "Notes on the History of English Copyright."
   c. "The Calendar": an essay and tables on the Julian and Gregorian calendars, saints' days and church feasts, and regnal years of the English monarchs.

M2. Hart, James D. With revisions and additions by Phillip W. Leininger. *The Oxford Companion to American Literature.* 6th ed. New York: Oxford University Press, 1995.

The *OCAL* is more circumscribed in its coverage than the *OCEL*, in that few foreign entries appear. Instead, Hart and Leininger (the latter of whom completed the volume after Hart's death) provide extensive cultural, social, and political background, reflecting the social-science orientation of many American literary studies.

Contents:

1. Authors: biographies and works with their dates;[1] data on foreign authors limited to their association with American literature.
2. Works: includes more than 1,100 summaries; some use of quotations.
3. Characters (fictional and historical).[2]

4. Literary terms, other than standard prosodic ones.
5. Literary schools and movements; also entries for literary awards, literary societies, scholarly organizations, magazines, newspapers, anthologies, book collectors, and printers.
6. Cultural background: "social, economic, aesthetic, scientific, military, political and religious subjects that have affected the actions and thoughts, and hence the writings, in the lands now forming the United States . . ." (Preface).
7. Appendix: Chronological Index [of literary and social history 1578-1994], pp. 751-79.[3]

Arrangement:

1. Alphabetical: no table of contents or index.
2. Cross-references indicated by a diamond symbol.
3. Appendix following dictionary proper, pp. 861-96.

Review Questions:

1. For which of the following would you expect to find entries: Isadora Duncan, the Mennonites, blank verse, the Algonquin Indians, Shakespeare, the Wizard of Oz, Horatio Alger, *The Saturday Evening Post*, transcendentalism, World War II, the Beat movement, Ralph Ellison's *Invisible Man*, the detective story, T. S. Eliot, Sherwood Anderson, *Leaves of Grass, Death of a Salesman*, chantey, Shaw's *Major Barbara*, Captain Ahab, Holden Caulfield, Scrooge, Tom Sawyer, free verse, realism, Jayne Anne Phillips?
2. Describe the difference in emphasis between the *OCEL* and *OCAL*.

Research Problems:

1. What are "gift books"? When were they popular? In which gift book were many of Hawthorne's *Twice-Told Tales* first published? Which of these tales is a moral allegory or parable dealing with man's isolation from his fellows and from God?
2. Who were the major twentieth-century Agrarian writers? In what did they believe? In what decades were the Agrarians active as a group?

3. When was *The Nation* founded, and who were some of its early 1980s contributors?
4. Identify briefly: A. S. W. Rosenbach, Brander Matthews, Frances Trollope.
5. Who is Benito Cerano? What happens to him? When was the work in which he appears first published? When did its author die?
6. Who coined the term "stream of consciousness"? Which three American authors are considered predecessors of the founder of this technique? Which American playwright used stream of consciousness?

Notes (*OCAL*)

1. Supplementary sources include *Benét's Reader's Encyclopedia of American Literature*, ed. George Perkins, Barbara Perkins, and Phillip Leininger (New York: HarperCollins, 1991); Gerald Bordman, *Oxford Companion to American Theatre*, 2nd ed. (New York: OUP, 1992); *Contemporary Authors* (M16); *The Penguin Companion to American Literature* (M12, headnote), and *The Oxford Companion to Women's Writing in the United States*, ed. Cathy N. Davidson and Linda Wagner-Martin (New York: OUP, 1995).
2. For folklore characters, also see Richard M. Dorson, ed. *Handbook of American Folklore* (Bloomington: Indiana UP, 1983).
3. For a book-length chronology, see *Annals of American Literature 1602-1983*, ed. Richard M. Ludwig and Clifford A. Nault, Jr. (New York: OUP, 1986).

M3. *A Literary History of England.* Ed. Albert C. Baugh. 2nd ed. New York: Appleton, 1967.

Unlike a handbook, a literary history is chronologically arranged and deals in some depth with the backgrounds of the various periods as well as with specific authors. If you wish to acquaint yourself with, say, Anglo-Saxon literature, you will find it more convenient to use Baugh than the *OCEL*; the subject is too broad for adequate treatment in a handbook. Baugh is still the standard one-volume history of English literature, striking a nice balance between detail and interpretation.

Note that although the second edition of Baugh updates the critical coverage through the mid-1960s, the literature surveyed is still limited to pre-World War II writings.[1]

Contents:

1. English literature from its beginnings to 1939.
2. French and Latin works written in England during the medieval period.
3. Irish and Scottish writers.
4. Ample use of quotation.
5. Philological, political, economic, and social background.
6. Bibliographical footnotes to standard editions and to significant biographical, critical, and historical books and articles.

Arrangement:

1. Identification of contributors opposite title page.[2]
2. Table of Contents: the "Books" reflect current periodization of English literature. These are further divided into parts and chapters; the latter often bear such broad titles as "The Spirit of the Restoration," "Aestheticism and Decadence," etc.
3. List of abbreviations of journals and other scholarly publications cited in the bibliographical footnotes, pp. xiv-xv.
4. Chronological survey by periods: the text proper.
5. Marginal subject headings on each page of the text.
6. Bibliographical as well as substantive footnotes on each page of the text; these bibliographical citations are to works written before 1948 (Baugh's first edition).
7. Bibliographical supplement following p. 1605 (secondary works written through the mid 1960s): "Throughout the text of this book, a point (.) set beside a page number indicates that references to new critical material [after 1948] will be found under an identical paragraph/page number [set in boldface] in the BIBLIOGRAPHICAL SUPPLEMENT" (Guide to Reference Marks).

Review Questions:

1. How does the arrangement of Baugh differ from that of the *OCEL*? Under what circumstances would you be compelled to begin your research with Baugh?
2. Where can you find bibliographical information in Baugh?
3. From when to when does the second edition update the 1948 edition in regard to primary works (works *by* the literary author)? In regard to secondary works (works *about* the literary author)?
4. How can you find bibliographical entries in the Supplement that continue the bibliographical discussion in the text proper?
5. What else is treated in Baugh aside from strictly literary concerns?

Research Problems:

1. In what respect was England "unique in the Europe of the year 1000"? What four factors made it so?
2. What historical "laws" of civilization does Toynbee attempt to discover in his *Studies of History*? Who were "the Webbs," and what bearing on literature does their work have? Cite one secondary study dealing with the Webbs.
3. Who were the three great novelists of the mid-eighteenth century, and what was each one's special gift to fiction? What is the most comprehensive modern literary history dealing with prose fiction of the mid-eighteenth century? What major studies of the eighteenth-century novel appeared in the 1950s?
4. Who was "a sort of Irish Poe" among the precursors of the Irish literary Renaissance? Who first popularized the legends of Cuchulain and Deirdre? Who edited *Poems and Ballads of Young Ireland*?
5. What were the philosophical and politico-military origins of the Aesthetic Movement in England? Where can Wilcox's article on *l'art pour l'art* be found? (Explain the periodical title abbreviation.)
6. In whose reign did the English court begin to encourage Anglo-Norman poets? To whom was the *Roman de Brut* dedicated? Cite a work published in 1924 that includes Philippe de Thaün's *Lapidary*.

Notes (Baugh)

1. Andrew Sanders's *The Short Oxford History of English Literature* (Oxford: Clarendon, 1994) provides coverage through post-modernism. Also useful for discussions of recent literature are *The Twentieth Century*, ed. Martin Dodsworth (New York: Penguin, 1994), volume 7 of the ten-volume Penguin History of Literature; A Guide to Twentieth Century Literature in English (S103) and *The Present*, ed. Boris Ford (Harmondsworth: Penguin, 1983), part of the excellent series The New Pelican Guide to English Literature.
2. The two-volume *A Critical History of English Literature*, 2nd ed. (New York: Ronald, 1970), written entirely by David Daiches, amply realizes the author's hope "that the pattern which a single mind imposes on this vast material will make my account more lively and suggestive than the conscientious composite works of reference by teams of experts . . ." (Preface). More recent alternatives are Harry Blamires, *A Short History of English Literature*, 2nd ed. (London: Methuen, 1984); and, under the same title, the second edition of Robert Barnard's survey (Oxford: Blackwell, 1994).

   Individual literary periods are given excellent book-length treatment in *The Oxford History of English Literature*, ed. F. P. Wilson et al., 16 vols. (Oxford: Clarendon, 1945-). Note that the Bedrick and Penguin works mentioned in note 1 above also provide book-length treatment of various literary periods. These works, however, are composed of collections of individually authored essays.

   Also see Ernest A. Baker, *The History of the English Novel*, 10 vols, 1924-39; rpt with an 11th vol. by Lionel Stevenson (New York: Barnes, 1967); Lionel Stevenson, *The English Novel: A Panorama* (Boston: Houghton, 1960); the in-progress *Cambridge History of Literary Criticism*, ed. Peter Brooks, H. B. Nisbet, and Claude Rawson, 9 vols. projected (Cambridge: CUP, 1989-); George Watson, *The Literary Critics* (S76); William K. Wimsatt, Jr. and Cleanth Brooks, *Literary Criticism: A Short History* (New York: Knopf, 1957); "The Rise of English" (chapter 1) in Terry Eagleton, *Literary Theory* (S131); and Elmer Borklund, *Contemporary Literary Critics*, 2nd. ed. (London: Macmillan, 1982), a discursive and evaluative bio-bibliographical guide to major English and American critics.

M4. *Columbia Literary History of the United States*. Ed. Emory Elliott. New York: Columbia University Press, 1988.

The *CLHUS* reflects the current view of American literature and society as a salad rather than a melting pot. Forgoing a "unifying vision of national identity," the editors seek out pluralism, devoting considerable space to ethnic and women writers, political writers, and theorists. The editors' definition of literature of the United States is admirable, being neither time bound, language bound, nor canon bound: "we mean all written and oral literary works produced in that part of the world that has become the United States of America" (xix).

Contents:

1. American literature from precolonial times to the present:
   a. pre-Columbian through 1987.
   b. works in languages other than English.
   c. works not previously recognized as significant.
2. Some quotation.
3. Broad cultural background essays, e.g., "Immigrants and Other Americans," "Culture, Power, and Society."
4. Period genre essays treating a number of writers, e.g., "[Colonial] Sermons and Theological Writings," "The Poetry of Colonial America."
5. Essays on particular major writers.[1]

Arrangement:

1. An important Preface and General Introduction.
2. Table of Contents: Five major parts, each subdivided into three or four subsidiary parts, totaling eighty-five discrete, signed essays.
3. Contributors' academic affiliation and major works, p. 1201.
4. Index of authors and subjects, p. 1211.

Review Questions:

1. What are the main differences between the *CLHUS* (Elliott) and the *OCAL*?
2. Are the *CLHUS* subchapters signed?
3. Which of the following would you expect to find discussed: science and technology in America, Irish-American literature, the *New Yorker* magazine, imagist poetry, Davy Crockett, jazz music, Alexander Hamilton, Dashiell Hammett, labor issues in fiction, Naturalism, gay drama, Jewish-American literature, T. S. Eliot's *Four Quartets*, Adrienne Rich?

Research Problems:

1. Quote a seven-word Sioux song. Who wrote the essay you are reading? Where does he teach, and which of his works won a Pulitzer prize?
2. Which scene in *Narrative of the Life of Frederick Douglass* is paralleled in almost all slave narratives? Which slave narrative by a woman does Carolyn Porter consider "the richest"?
3. How does Elaine Kim classify the genre of Maxine Hong Kingston's *The Woman Warrior*? Why do the Nisei in John Okada's novel envy the veteran who lost his leg? What aesthetic fault does Kim find with the female characters in Okada's novel?
4. Which American science-fiction pulp writers possess a first-rate literary imagination, according to Larry McCaffrey?
   How does Laurie Anderson "decharacterize" herself?
5. What did Lionel Trilling have to say about *Hamlet*? In which decades did Trilling gain his reputation? Who wrote the essay you are drawing on, and where does he teach?
6. How does the name "Mark Twain" differ from pen names used by earlier English writers? Whose critical insight is this, and what is the title of the full-length book he has written?

Notes (*CLHUS*)

1. Since this volume lacks notes and a bibliography, the editors refer you to *The Literary History of the United States: Bibliography*

(M6), *American Literary Scholarship* (S34), and the *Modern Language Association International Bibliography* (M7). The multi-volumed *New Cambridge History of American Literature*, ed. Sacvan Berkovich (Cambridge UP, 1994), is important as an alternative or supplement to the *CLHUS*, since Berkovich and his five contributors treat diversity issues as more systemic than does Elliott. (To date, two volumes have appeared covering the years 1590 through 1865.) It should be noted, however, that Elliott's later work, *The Columbia History of the American Novel* (New York: Columbia UP, 1991), includes literature of South as well as North America and rejects the ghettoization of non-mainstream voices.

For a more manageable one-volume literary history, see volume 9 of the *New Pelican Guide to English Literature*, 9 vols. (Harmondsworth, Middlesex: Penguin, 1982-88), which treats American literature; and Marcus Cunliffe, *The Literature of the United States*, 4th ed. (New York: Penguin, 1986). Cunliffe has also edited two volumes in The History of Literature in the English Language series: *American Literature to 1900* (1973) and *American Literature Since 1900* (1975). Also see Basler, Roy P., ed. *Guide to the Study of the United States of America: Representative Books Reflecting the Development of American Life and Thought* (Washington, DC: Library of Congress, 1960), *Supplement* (1976); Robert J. Di Pietro and Edward Ifkovic, eds., *Ethnic Perspectives in American Literature: Selected Essays on the European Contribution* (New York: MLA, 1983); Wimsatt and Brooks's *Literary Criticism: A Short History* (M3,n.2); and Borklund's *Contemporary Literary Critics* (M3,n.2).

For a comparative literature counterpart of the *Columbia Literary History of the United States* consult Werner Paul Friederich, *Outline of Comparative Literature from Dante Alighieri to Eugene O'Neill* (Chapel Hill: U of North Carolina P, 1954). More introduction than history, but less dated is Ulrich Weisstein, *Comparative Literature and Literary Theory*, trans. William Riggan (Bloomington: Indiana UP, 1973), with supplements in German. A Comparative History of Literature in European Languages, an in-progress series founded by the International Comparative Literature Association, offers entire volumes devoted to a particular topic (e.g., Expressionism, Symbolism).

M5. *The New Cambridge Bibliography of English Literature.* Ed. George Watson [Vols. 1-3], I. R. Willison [Vol. 4], and J. D. Pickles [Vol. 5, Index]. Cambridge: Cambridge University Press, 1969-1977.

The *New CBEL* is the starting place for any serious research into English literature.[1] This work is a vast—though selective—primary and secondary bibliography; that is, it lists works *by* the author and works *about* the author and his canon. The *New CBEL* treats British writers whose reputations were established by 1950; critical coverage for all writers is now virtually up to date. Despite its modernity, however, the *New CBEL* will never entirely supersede its predecessor because it omits much of the intellectual, political, and social background material included in F. W. Bateson's great pioneer effort, the *CBEL*.[2]

Contents:

1. Writers native to or mainly resident in the British Isles.
2. Writers whose reputations were established by 1950; also includes works written after 1950 by authors established prior to that date.
3. Primary bibliography of works in book form; generally excludes short pamphlets and contributions to periodicals and miscellanies except in the case of the most prominent literary figures.[3]
4. Primary bibliographies include works in both English and Latin.
5. Indication of further unlisted works.
6. Intellectual, political, and social background:
   a. representative works by historians, theologians, philosophers, scholars, and scientists.
   b. representative ephemeral literature—i.e., political and controversial pamphlets, anonymous and pseudonymous squibs,[4] mock-biographies, etc.
   c. representative literary bypaths—i.e., letter-writing, sport, oratory, travel, and law.
7. History of printing and publishing; newspapers and magazines.
8. Manuscripts up to A.D.1500.
9. First editions: number of volumes, place of publication (if other than London), date.
10. Dates of extant editions and translations up to fifty years from the first.

11. Details of the more important or convenient modern editions and reprints, both collected and individual.
12. Selected secondary books and articles in all languages by critics of all nationalities.[5]

Arrangement:

1. Chronological: Vol. 1—Anglo-Saxon, Middle English, Renaissance to Restoration; Vol. 2—Restoration to Romantic Revival; Vol. 3—the Nineteenth Century; Vol. 4—The Twentieth Century; Vol. 5—Master Index.
2. Detailed Table of Contents for each volume.
3. List of Contributors and Abbreviations at front of each volume.
4. General Introduction, Vol. 1: bibliographies, histories, anthologies, prosodic and linguistic studies.
5. Introductions to each period.
6. Subdivisions into genres or literary topics within each period, i.e., Fiction, Scottish Literature, etc.
7. Further subdivision into individual authors within each genre: bibliographies, collected editions, separate works, secondary studies; heading number 1 denotes primary bibliography, heading number 2 secondary.
8. Primary bibliography—the author's canon—usually in a single chronological list.
9. Secondary bibliography for the entire canon in a single chronological list.[6]
10. Provisional indexes of primary authors and some subjects at the end of each volume.
11. Volume 5, the master index, is more inclusive than the provisional indexes with regard to periodical titles, extra-literary authors, and foreign secondary authors.[7] (Pseudonyms appear in inverted commas in both the provisional indexes and the master index.)

Review Questions:

1. To appear in the *New CBEL*, by what year must an author's reputation have been established?
2. Why is Bateson's *CBEL* still worth consulting?
3. Do American authors appear in the *New CBEL*? American critics?

4. Mention some off-literary subjects covered in the *NEW CBEL.*
5. In which part of which volume of the *NEW CBEL* can you find bibliographies of works on grammar, syntax, and vocabulary?
6. Under what period and subject headings would you expect to find the bibliography of *Beowulf*? Of the Globe playhouse?
7. Would you find an entry for *Paradise Lost* in the index?

Research Problems:

1. What is the subject of Stephen Gosson's *The Schoole of Abuse*? When was it first printed? Cite another work by Gosson. How many editions of this work were published in the sixteenth century?
2. Cite an anthology devoted to five plays by Peter Ustinov. Which plays does it contain? How many unpublished plays by Ustinov does Willison list? Cite a critical work on Ustinov.
3. Who translated Henryson's *The Testament of Cresseid* into modern English in 1945? In what work does E. M. W. Tillyard discuss *The Testament*?
4. What did Marco Polo entitle his travel book? When was it first published? When was it first translated into English? Who edited the first twentieth-century English edition?
5. During what years was *The Heartsease Library of High Class Fiction* issued? Under what title was *Great Thoughts from Master Minds* continued? Who were the assistant editors of *The Egoist* between 1914 and 1919?
6. List four English-language critical works dealing with Hugo von Hofmannsthal's influence on English literature.

Notes (*New CBEL*)

1. Also see Howard-Hill's *Bibliography of British Literary Bibliographies* (S32); and *Shakespearian Bibliography and Textual Criticism* (S32, passim); Larry S. Champion, *The Essential Shakespeare: An Annotated Bibliography of Major Modern Studies*, 2nd ed. (Boston: G. K. Hall, 1993) is an extensively annotated bibliography of important twentieth-century Shakespeare criticism. Also see Thompson's *Motif-Index of Folk Literature* (S16); the "guides to

research" on Romantic, Victorian, and Anglo-Irish literature published under the auspices of the Modern Language Association; and the Reference Guides to Literature series published by G. K. Hall. For reference materials, see Bracken's *Reference Works in British and American Literature* (S2). Michael Marcuse (my Preface) includes lists of major British authors for whom bibliographies are provided, p. 267. For the comparative literature counterpart of the *New CBEL*, see Baldensperger and Friederich's *Bibliography of Comparative Literature* (S49).

2. *The Cambridge Bibliography of English Literature*, ed. F. W. Bateson, 4 vols. (Cambridge: CUP, 1940); and *Supplement: A.D. 600-1900* [Vol. 5 of *CBEL*], ed. George Watson (Cambridge: CUP, 1957). The original work included the literatures of India, South Africa, Canada, Australia, and New Zealand as well as background bibliographies on science, economics, law, and classical and oriental scholarship. However, other extra-literary sections have been retained and updated. Note that the 1900-1950 volume contains extensive material on book production and distribution, theatre as a mass medium, writers on off-literary subjects, and newspapers and magazines.
3. Keep in mind that despite their size, both the *CBEL* and *New CBEL* are selective bibliographies. The list of works by a minor author may not always be complete. Moreover, entries for works by a minor author may be dispersed under various headings without cross-references, making the use of indexes essential.
4. For anonyma and pseudonyma, also see Halkett and Laing's *Dictionary* (S4), the *National Union Catalog* (M22), the *British Library General Catalogue* (S44), and Pollard and Redgrave's *Short-Title Catalogue* (M23), including those works listed under M23, n.2, which comprise the English national bibliography.
5. For Biography, also consult the *Dictionary of National Biography* (M14).
6. Unfortunately, secondary material is not classified according to the particular primary work or subject treated, as was the editorial practice for the *CBEL*; for example, in order to find studies dealing with "In Memoriam," you must scan all nineteen pages of Tennyson criticism.
7. Consult the master index first to find the period volume for bibliographies of unfamiliar authors.

M6. *Literary History of the United States: Bibliography.* Ed. Robert Spiller et al. 4th ed., rev. New York: Macmillan, 1974.

Although Spiller's companion volume to the *LHUS: Bibliography*, the *LHUS: History*, has been largely displaced by the more recent *Columbia Literary History of the United States* (M4), the *LHUS Bibliography* is still the best initial source for research in American literature. If not quite the "guide to the *present* state of resources and scholarship in American literary culture" that we would wish (Preface, my italics), it remains an important compendium of discursive, selective primary and secondary bibliographies of books, periodical items, monograph studies, technical and textual studies, and bibliographies for the specialist.

To use the *LHUS: Bibliography* and its incorporated supplements with facility, you should know something about Spiller's successive additions. The original bibliography was published in 1948. In 1959 the first bibliographical supplement appeared covering the decade 1949-58; in 1972 *Supplement II* appeared covering 1959-1970. The fourth revised edition of the *LHUS: Bibliography*, while one inclusive volume, is only partially cumulated. Although the volume has a single table of contents and index and is continuously paginated, it is still arranged in the order of its initial compilation: the first supplement follows the original work; the second supplement follows the first.

Contents:

1. Coverage through 1970, in some cases 1971.
2. Guide to Resources: library holdings in American literary culture throughout the United States, catalogs, directories, union lists, special collections; guides to reference books, theses, and other professional studies; registries of publication of books, periodicals, and newspapers; biographical and reference dictionaries and digests; sources for cultural history.
3. Bibliographies of Literature and Culture: general—periodicals, clubs, histories, movements; specific—by period and type (colonial through twentieth century; folk literature; Indian lore; popular literature).
4. Movements and Influences: literature of travel and westward migration; non-English writing in America; regionalism and local color throughout the United States; science and social criticism;

literature of slavery and the Civil War; transcendentalism and utopianism; escapism and aestheticism; American writers and books abroad.

5. Bibliographies of authors: information on separate and collected works, edited texts and reprints, biography and criticism, primary sources (including manuscript location in public depositories), and secondary bibliographies; primary sources are selective with respect to separates, magazine pieces, and ephemera.[1]

Arrangement:

1. Cumulated, detailed Table of Contents, pp. xi-xxvii.
2. Key to Abbreviations, pp. xxviii-xxxviii.
3. The 1948 bibliography, pp. 3-790.
4. The 1959 bibliography, pp. 793-1033.
5. The 1972 bibliography, pp. 1037-1375.
6. Cumulated index: at end of second supplement, pp. 1377-1466. Entries for names of literary authors, major critics, titles, and subjects;[2] cross-references in both index and text.

Review Questions:

1. Until what year does the fourth revised edition of the *LHUS: Bibliography* extend its coverage?
2. What is meant by a "Guide to Resources"?
3. Why are three page references often given for a subject in the table of contents?

Research Problems:

1. What general holdings of the Henry E. Huntington Library in San Marino, California, would interest a researcher concerned with American literary culture? Name a work by a major nineteenth-century New England writer that was edited in 1960 from a manuscript in the Huntington Library. Name a directory that indexes special collections in libraries throughout the United States and that is regularly revised and updated.
2. List three comprehensive bibliographies published in 1970-71 of black history and culture in America. Cite a compilation of black

songs of World War I. In what work can you find evaluations by black writers of William Styron's *The Confessions of Nat Turner*?

3. Cite two twentieth-century studies of women's education in the nineteenth century. Cite three anthologies compiled in the nineteenth century of American women writers. What work contains the conclusions reached by the U.S. President's Commission on the Status of Women?
4. Which two works by Edmund Wilson were significant contributions to the analytical and aesthetic movement in twentieth-century criticism? Name three English critics who have written important analytical studies of American literature.
5. What are dime novels, and what superseded them? Who is the hero of what has "probably been the most lucrative continuation of the dime-novel tradition in the twentieth century"? Cite a bibliography of dime novels compiled in 1964.
6. What seven works offer the cultural historian insight into domestic relations in colonial New England?

Notes (*LHUS: Bibliography*)

1. Also see Blanck's *Bibliography of American Literature* (M21); Nilon's *Bibliography of Bibliographies in American Literature* (S40); Bracken's *Reference Works in British and American Literature* (S2); Leary's *Articles on American Literature* (S40); *American Literary Scholarship* (S34); Woodress's *Eight American Authors* (S41); Harbert and Rees's *Fifteen American Authors Before 1900* (S38); Bryer's *Sixteen Modern American Authors* (S36); Philip M. White, *American Indian Studies: A Bibliographic Guide* (Englewood, CO: Libraries Unlimited, 1995); M. Thomas Inge, Maurice Duke, and Jackson R. Bryer, eds., *Black American Writers: Bibliographical Essays*, 2 vols. (New York: St. Martin's, 1978); Duke, Bryer, and Inge's *American Women Writers: Bibliographical Essays* (Westport, CT: Greenwood, 1983): Gohdes's *Bibliographical Guide* (S37); Jones and Ludwig's *Guide* (S5); the serial bibliographies, now discontinued, in the journal *American Literature* (M19,n.7); the Reference Guides to Literature series published by G. K. Hall; and the four-volume *Facts on File*

series published by G. K. Hall; and the four-volume *Facts on File Bibliography of American Fiction* (New York: Facts on File, 1991) that includes primary and secondary coverage from 1588 through 1988. See Michael Marcuse (my Preface), who includes lists of major American authors for whom bibliographies are provided, p. 382.

For the comparative literature counterpart of the *LHUS: Bibliography*, see Baldensperger and Friederich's *Bibliography of Comparative Literature* (S43).

2. "For each author who is given an individual bibliography, the main entry is italicized. These authors are indicated by an asterisk before the surname" (Index).

M7. *MLA International Bibliography of Books and Articles on the Modern Languages and Literatures*. New York: MLA, 1922-.

The *MLA International Bibliography* is an annual, non-cumulative catalog of secondary works only, by critics of all nationalities about literary authors of all nationalities. Its functions are 1) to update other bibliographies and 2) to provide wide secondary coverage. The *MLAIB* can be computer-searched.

First published in 1922 as part of the scholarly journal *PMLA* (Publications of the Modern Language Association of America), it was originally called "American Bibliography" because only American scholarship was entered. The bibliography for 1956, still part of *PMLA*, appeared under a new title, "Annual Bibliography," to reflect a major policy change: the listing of secondary works by scholars of all nationalities. The current title dates from the bibliography for 1963, the current format from the bibliography for 1981, when computerization allowed for a subject index to supplement the classified listings, enhancing the usefulness of the bibliography. Both the Classified Listings and the Subject index should be used for all searches. The *1993 MLAIB* is described below.[1]

Contents (Volumes 1-5: Classified Listings with Author Index):

1. Subject coverage: Vol. 1—British, Irish, Australian, English-Canadian, New Zealand, English Caribbean, and American literatures. Vol. 2—European,[2] Latin American, Asian, Austronesian, and African literatures. Vol. 3—Linguistics. Vol. 4—General Literature and Related Topics (includes film and literary theory).[3] Vol. 5—Folklore.
2. Secondary works only: articles, essays, monographs, book-length studies, anthologies (i.e., Festschriften and other analyzed collections),[4] scholarly editions, and dissertations—if abstracted in *DAI* (M25) or published. Also included are films, records, microforms, and invented language works of a secondary nature.[5]
3. Scholars of all nationalities represented.
4. Annual lists; coverage of current scholarship usually within two years;[6] however, the CD-ROM database eliminates the time lag of the printed volumes.
5. Index to authors of secondary material.

Arrangement (Classified Listings):

1. Guide for Users of the *1993 MLAIB.*
2. Master List of Periodicals in Acronym Order.
3. Guide to Classified Listings (a brief table of contents preceding each volume).
4. Divisions of each section arranged from the most general to the most narrow. Subdivisions within the national literatures first by period, then alphabetically by author. The divisions of volumes 3, 4, and 5 and their subdivisions, when not arbitrary, are also alphabetical.
5. Catalog style: unannotated entries (after early issues) except for titles requiring explanation.[7] But the subject descriptors in the bibliographies for 1981 and thereafter serve, in effect, as minimal annotations.
6. Itemized entries: each entry is preceded by a bracketed Arabic item number; the volume number (see Contents #1) is understood. Following the bibliographical citation[8] there may be bracketed descriptors having to do with the genres, subjects, themes, approaches, influences, comparisons, etc. with which the secondary

work is concerned. A dagger symbol precedes those descriptors used in the Classified Listings (i.e., for *shifts of perspective*, see the keyword *perspective*, not *shifts*).

7. MLA Document Author Index, Volumes 1-5, 1993: all secondary authors, editors, illustrators, translators, cited in the Classified Listings.[9] An entry number in parentheses is a duplicate in another volume of the entry preceding it.

Contents and Arrangement (Volumes 1-5: Subject Index):

1. Indexes documents in vols. 1-5 of the Classified Listings by individuals, languages, groups, genres, style, structure, subjects, sources and influences, processes, methodology, theoretical schools, etc.
2. Alphabetical arrangement.
3. Cross-references to names used by *MLAIB* (Abélard for Abailard), to narrower and related terms, and to other entries in the Classified Listings.
4. As in the Classified Listings, an entry number in parentheses is a duplicate in another volume of the entry preceding it.

Review Questions:

1. How often does the *MLA International Bibliography* appear? Is it cumulative? Is it annotated? In what sense was it always "international"? Why was it called "American Bibliography" prior to 1956?
2. Which volume of the *MLAIB* five-volume Classified Listings is of particular interest to students of American literature? To students of German literature?
3. For which of the following would you expect to find entries: a collection of critical essays on Christian literary criticism, an unedited commercial reprint of *An American Tragedy*, an English translation of Icelandic poetry, an article on the etymology of "mumbo-jumbo"? Would you expect to find a listing of works by Ernest Hemingway?
4. How does the *MLA International Bibliography* supplement the *NEW CBEL* and the *LHUS: Bibliography*?
5. How can you ascertain how prolific a particular scholar is?

Research Problems:

1. Which two West Asian literatures appear to have attracted the most critical attention in 1993? How many entries are listed for each of the two countries?
2. How many entries for *Hamlet* do you find in the *PMLA* American Bibliography for 1921? In the *1992 MLAIB* Classified Listings? Suggest two or three factors to account for the increase. How does the style of the 1921 bibliography differ from that of the bibliographies of the 1980s?
3. Cite complete publication information for two *1992 MLAIB* entries on the treatment of widows in French literature of the seventeenth and eighteenth centuries, respectively.
4. How many works (including dissertations) on John Ashbery are listed in the *1992 MLAIB*? How many could you have found easily without using the Subject Index volume?
5. Discover what is discussed in the following articles without consulting the articles themselves: Carl A. Swanson, "Ibsen and the *Comédie-Française*," *SS* 19 (1946): 70-78; and Keith Cushman, "A Reading of Joyce Carol Oates's 'Four Summers'" *SSF* 18.2 (1981): 137-46.
6. Cite a piece of literary criticism written by Ho Chi Minh in 1975. Which of his poems were translated into English in 1977, and where can they be found? (Explain abbreviations.)

Notes (*MLAIB*)

1. Bibliographies for earlier years may differ with regard to subjects covered and details of arrangement. The 1921-68 bibliographies have been reprinted under separate cover by the Kraus Reprint Corporation and by New York University Press.
2. Criticism of classical Greek and Latin works is excluded. Within the European section, arrangement is by geographical region—Central, Northern, and Southern Europe. Eastern Europe is grouped with Central Asia and Siberia.
3. For works about film, use the Classified Listings, vol. 4: General Literature and Related Topics—Film. Note also that the *MLAIB* is the most extensive source for theory. Again, use the Classified

Listings, vol. 4: General Literature and Related Topics. The subheading Literary Theory is divided into deconstructionist, feminist, formalist, hermeneutic, linguistic, Marxist, narrative, phenomenological, philosophical, postmodernist, poststructuralist, psychoanalytic, psychological, reader-response, reception, rhetorical, semiotic, sociological, and structuralist.

4. A Festschrift is an anthology of essays offered as a tribute to an eminent scholar. An analyzed collection is one whose contents are described on its Library of Congress card.
5. Excluded are book reviews (but not review articles), most translations and non-scholarly editions, and strictly pedagogical works. Book reviews can be found in the *Annual Bibliography of English Language and Literature* (S35), the *MLAIB*'s British counterpart; in the *Arts and Humanities Citation Index* (S51); and in the *Humanities Index* (S57).
6. Thus, to prepare a listing of works published in 1980, you would have to consult the bibliographies for 1980 and 1981; you might consult the 1982 bibliography as well, since occasionally a work will elude the bibliographer for even longer than one year. For complete and current coverage, depending on your subject, the following works might be relevant: *Annual Bibliography of English Language and Literature* (S35), especially for British subjects; more generally, *The Year's Work in English Studies* (S42); *The Year's Work in Modern Language Studies* (S47); *Index to Little Magazines* (S58); *Index to Commonwealth Little Magazines* (S56); *Index to American Little Magazines* (S55); *Comprehensive Index to English-Language Little Magazines* (S64); *Alternative Press Index* (S50); *The Left Index* (S59); *Humanities Index* (S57); *British Humanities Index* (S53); *Essay and General Literature Index* (M27); *Arts and Humanities Citation Index* (S51); and the most recent of the specialized bibliographies appearing in scholarly periodicals (M19).
7. However, from 1971 through 1975, an asterisk after an entry indicated that a 200-word abstract of that article could be found in *MLA Abstracts*, now discontinued. For other abstracts of current criticism, see M25,n.1.
8. Note that volume numbers of journals appear in Arabic numerals, and that prior to the *1981 MLAIB*, undated items are understood to have been published in the year of the bibliography.

9. From 1964 through 1980 the secondary author index is found at the end of each volume; it lists contributors' names only, followed by the item numbers of their works.

M8. *The Oxford English Dictionary.* 2nd ed. Prepared by J. A. Simpson and E. S. C. Weiner. 20 vols. Oxford: Clarendon, 1989.

The Oxford English Dictionary Additions Series. Ed. John Simpson and Edmund Weiner. Oxford: Clarendon Press, 1993-.

The new edition of the *OED* is the culmination of more than a century's labor by thousands of lexicographers. This national linguistic project was initiated in 1857, its purpose being to trace the *history* of "the words that have formed the English vocabulary from the time of the earliest records down to the present day, with all the relevant facts concerning their form, sense-history, pronunciation, and etymology" (1: vii). Some 59 million words are entered in the current *OED*; dated quotations with exact bibliographical references illustrate each change of meaning.

The second edition integrates the original twelve volumes (1888-1928) edited by James Murray and his colleagues, the 1933 supplement, and the four-volume supplement (1972-86) edited by R. W. Burchfield. Simpson and Weiner include new vocabulary as well as revisions and corrections of previous entries. In 1993, the publication of two volumes, each covering A through Z words, initiated the *Oxford English Dictionary Additions Series*. The *Series* is designed to provide readers with access to the third in-progress edition. Every two years or so, another volume will appear, containing new words and supplementary meanings for words already listed in the second edition. The final pages of volume 2 comprise a cumulative index to the series. The *OED* is also available on CD-ROM.

Contents:

1. Standard words: current, obsolete (unless obsolete by 1150), archaic.

2. The main technical and scientific vocabularly of the English language.
3. Some dialect (especially before 1500), adopted foreign words, and slang.[1]
4. Cross references.
5. Dated quotations illustrating changes in meaning.

Arrangement:

1. Introduction discussing differences between this edition and earlier volumes.
2. General Explanations: especially important is the material on classification of the vocabulary (1: xxv-xxxii).[2]
3. The History of the *OED*.
4. Key to the Conventions of the Dictionary. Be sure to look at this section.
5. The dictionary proper: division into main words and, in smaller type, subordinate words or combinations and derivatives; these are generally listed in a single alphabet with subordinate words (usually variant or obsolete forms) and combinations (e.g., Black Jack) concluding the main entry.
6. Identification of each main entry word: main form, pronunciation, part of speech, specification by field to which it is related (e.g., music, astronomy), variety of English to which it belongs if not standard British (Canadian, Australian, etc.), and status.
7. Etymology and form history: derivation, subsequent changes, miscellaneous historical facts.
8. Signification or senses: definitions and dated quotations.[3]
9. The Bibliography at end of volume 20. This section begins with an explanatory note and a list of abbreviations used in the Bibliography.
10. The Bibliography proper: fuller author-title-date entries for quotations. See Volume 1, xxx for explanation of the Bibliography format.

Review Questions:

1. What unique feature of the *OED* distinguishes it from other dictionaries?

2. When was the original *OED* begun?
3. Does the current edition include Americanisms?
4. What's a subordinate word? What format device is used to identify it?
5. Quotations from most of Christopher Marlowe's works are cited in the *OED*. In consequence, would the Bibliography enumerate his entire canon?

Research Problems:

1. Define "blarney" as a transitive and as an intransitive verb. What is its origin and status? What is the first recorded example of its use as a verb? (Note author's name—given as well as surname—work, dates of composition and publication.) Where and when did Goldsmith and Scott use "blarney" as a noun?
2. Gloss the italicized words: "Away you *Scullion* . . . I'le *tickle* your *catastrophe*." In what play does this phrase appear?
3. What is the full title of the work in which "gaol" was first used as a transitive verb meaning to confine in a jail?
4. When was "neck" first used as a verb meaning to embrace? Quote the sentence. Under what word did you find it?
5. From whom did Freud borrow the concept of the id? From whom was Freud's source borrowing? Who was the translator responsible for creating the English word "id"?
6. When and in whose work did "herstory" enter the language?

Notes (*OED*)

1. Slang, sexual expressions, and "the written English of North America, Australia, New Zealand, South Africa, India, Pakistan and other regions" are prominent (xlviii). Also see the *Dictionary of American English on Historical Principles*, ed. William A. Craigie and James R. Hulbert, 4 vols. (Chicago: U of Chicago P, 1938-44) and the *Dictionary of Americanisms on Historical Principles*, ed. Mitford M. Mathews, 2 vols. (Chicago: U of Chicago P, 1951). Additional coverage is provided by *Words and Phrases Index: A Guide to Antedatings, New Words, New Com--pounds, New Meanings, and Other Published Scholarship Supple-*

menting the Oxford English Dictionary, Dictionary of Americanisms, Dictionary of American English and Other Major Dictionaries of the English Language, comp. C. Edward Wall and Edward Przebienda, 4 vols. (Ann Arbor: Pierian, 1969-70). Since the *WPI* merely locates scholarly discussions of words, you must also consult the periodical sources to which you are referred.

Also see *The American Heritage Dictionary* (S18), *Webster's New Dictionary of Synonyms* (S21); *Roget's International Thesaurus*, 5th ed., Robert L. Chapman, ed. (New York: HarperCollins, 1992); Casey Miller and Kate Swift, *The Handbook of Nonsexist Writing*, 2nd ed. (New York: Harper, 1988); Eric A. Partridge, *A Dictionary of Slang and Unconventional English: Colloquialisms and Catch-Phrases, Solecisms and Catachreses, Nick-names, Vulgarisms, and such Americanisms as have been Naturalized*, ed. Paul Beale, 8th ed. (New York: Macmillan, 1984); and A. J. Bliss, *A Dictionary of Foreign Words and Phrases in Current English*, (London: Routledge, 1983).

Academic writers in the humanities are most often asked to follow the conventions detailed in the *MLA Handbook* (S19) or *The Chicago Manual of Style* (S19). Clarification is provided by Kate Turabian, *A Manual for Writers of Term Papers, Theses, and Dissertations*, 6th ed., rev. John Grossman and Alice Bennett (Chicago: U of Chicago P, 1996).

2. For further clarification, see Donna Lee Berg, *A Guide to the Oxford English Dictionary* (Oxford: OUP, 1993). John Willinsky, *Empire of Words: The Reign of the OED* (Princeton: Princeton UP, 1994), offers a critique of the *OED* and its continuing revisions.
3. It is *not* customary to cite volume and page references for the *OED*.

CHAPTER 2

DICTIONARIES, HANDBOOKS, AND GUIDES

M9. *A Handbook to Literature*

M10. *Encyclopedia of Contemporary Literary Theory*

M11. *The Oxford Classical Dictionary*

M12. *Penguin Companion to Literature: European*

M13. *Guide to Reference Books*

M14. *Dictionary of National Biography*

M15. *Who's Who*

M16. *Contemporary Authors*

Chapter 2 introduces a number of works dealing with literary terms and theory, foreign literature, reference tools, and biography. All but the *Guide to Reference Books* are alphabetically arranged and, consequently, can be used with ease. One cannot, however, stress the value of this *Guide* too strongly; familiarity with it is as rewarding to students of literature as to librarians. The last three entries have been chosen for the way in which each answers a special need. Capsule biographies of well-known figures can be found in handbooks and encyclopedias; full-length biographies can be located through bibliographies. But for extensive scholarly biographical sketches of Britishers no longer living, the *DNB* is unrivaled. *Who's Who* and *Contemporary Authors*, the former mainly British in coverage, the latter American, are especially valuable for their biographical data on figures not yet sufficiently famous to have become the subject of a "life."

M9. Holman, C. Hugh, and William Harmon. *A Handbook to Literature*. 7th ed. Upper Saddle River, NJ: Prentice Hall, 1992.

This edition, based on the 1939 "Thrall and Hibbard," is still the standard literary handbook used in American universities. The orientation is both critical and historical with entries for terms broadly relevant to British and American literature. *A Handbook to Literature*, a paperback volume, would make a worthwhile addition to your personal library; the omitted information—biographies, plot summaries, and characters—is easily accessible elsewhere.

Contents:

1. Literary terms, many from classical rhetoric, new schools of literary criticism, and film criticism.[1]
2. Literary forms.
3. Some common literary allusions.[2]
4. Literary schools and movements.
5. Major literary periodicals and prizes.
6. Some bibliographic suggestions, these indicated as References.
7. Chronological outline of the literary history of English-speaking people, with British and American events entered side by side, to facilitate comparison.
8. Appendices: Nobel prizes for Literature; Pulitzer prizes for Fiction, Poetry, and Drama.

Arrangement:

1. To the User: Contains List of Abbreviations used in the text proper, p. ix.
2. Alphabetical; no table of contents or index of terms.
3. Cross-references: in small capitals in the body of the article; preceded by "See . . ." at end of the article.
4. Explanations of abbreviations used in the chronological outline, p. 552.
5. Appendices.
6. An Index of Proper Names of "all actual persons mentioned in the handbook proper" (ix) with the titles of the entries under which they can be found.

Review Questions:

1. Does Holman provide biographical entries? Entries for individual works?
2. What reference work supplements Holman's chronological outline of American literary history with an outline of political and scientific events?
3. For which of the following would you expect to find entries: existential criticism, erotic literature, dead metaphor, frontier literature, sonnet, *The Dial* (a periodical featuring American transcendentalist works)?

Research Problems:

1. Which English literary works were published in the following years: 1557, 1638, 1846? Name the Anglo-American writer who died in 1965.
2. What is a "curtal sonnet"? Describe its form and rhyme scheme. Name a well-known curtal sonnet.
3. Explain the nature of the "profile" as a literary type. Where did the term originate?
4. Who won the Pulitzer prizes for Fiction in the 1970s? For which works did they win the awards?
5. Name two writers associated with each type: the novel of incident, the novel of the soil, and the well-made novel.

6. Which critics are specifically associated with archetypal and phenomenological criticism? Name a structuralist critic.

Notes (Holman and Harmon)

1. Reliable alternatives are Chris Baldick, *The Concise Oxford Dictionary of Literary Terms* (Oxford: OUP, 1990), a slim volume with a useful pronunciation guide; J. A. Cudden, *A Dictionary of Literary Terms and Literary Theory*, 3rd ed. (Oxford: Blackwell, 1991); and Leonard Orr, *A Dictionary of Critical Theory* (S110), these last two dictionaries providing significant coverage of foreign material.
2. More allusions can be found in the fourth (1969) edition of the *Oxford Companion to English Literature* (M1).

M10. *Encyclopedia of Contemporary Literary Theory: Approaches, Scholars, Terms*. Ed. Irena R. Makaryk. Toronto: University of Toronto Press, 1993.

Literary theory informs virtually all serious critical analyses being written today, and Professor Makaryk's compilation of work by 170 scholars helps to make those analyses accessible. The *Encyclopedia*'s subtitle corresponds to its tripartite division; each section, including the last on literary terms, contains extensive current bibliographies.

Contents:

1. Approaches: 48 signed essays on various schools and concerns (i.e., archetypal criticism, Black criticism, cultural materialism), the contexts out of which they developed, the issues they address, and representative theorists.
2. Scholars: essays "not only [on] literary theorists and critics but also historians, philosophers, linguists, social scientists, theologians, polemicists, authors" (Introduction, viii). Some biographical background.

3. Terms: Brief essays on more than one hundred of the most important, frequently used, and most difficult concepts.[1]

Arrangement:

1. List of contributors, their universities, and the subjects of their *Encyclopedia* entries ([xi]-xiv).
2. Alphabetical within each division.
3. Cross-references indicated by "see" or asterisk.
4. Bibliographies, often divided into primary and secondary, follow each entry in all three divisions.[2]
5. Alphabetically arranged lists of the entries in each division, in lieu of an index.

Review Questions:

1. For which of the following would you expect to find entries: semiotics, feminist criticism, the Baroque, Longinus, Mikhail Bakhtin, Michel Foucault, Walter Pater, high seriousness, discourse, the canon?
2. Aside from signed essays, what other important feature does Makaryk provide?

Research Problems:

1. For whom was "the role of a sign . . . to represent, to stand as a *substitute* for something else"? What is the full title of the work in which the quoted statement appears? To what works did Roland Barthes contribute essays on Benveniste?
2. What production can be considered the "symbolic birthplace" of performance criticism? Who wrote the essay upon which you are drawing? With what university is the writer affiliated?
3. How does Hayden White oppose the notion of history as an objective discipline modeled after science? Where was he educated? What is the full title of his major work?
4. Name two African American critics of special significance to postcolonial scholars interested in the issue of subject positions. What does the Harvard critic hold with regard to subject positions?

5. From whom is the concept of liminality ultimately derived? Name three scholars who have written on liminality in Shakespeare. In what works? On whose discussion are you drawing?
6. Name the theoretician who developed and popularized the concept of the narratee? Which of his works is regarded as his most important achievement? How is the narratee constructed when the text is addressed to a collectivity?

Notes (Makaryk)

1. Also valuable is *Critical Terms for Literary Study*, ed. Frank Lentricchia and Thomas McLaughlin, 2nd ed. (Chicago: U of Chicago P, 1995), signed essays with brief bibliographies; and Michael Groden and Martin Kreiswirth, eds., *The Johns Hopkins Guide to Literary Theory and Criticism* (Baltimore: Johns Hopkins UP, 1994). For more succinct definitions, see Jeremy Hawthorn, *A Concise Glossary of Contemporary Literary Theory* (London: Arnold, 1992).
2. For more recent work, see the *MLA International Bibliography* (M7) and *The Year's Work in English Studies* (S42). Recent subject bibliographies can be found in *Introduction to Scholarship in Modern Languages and Literatures*, 2nd ed., ed. Joseph Gibaldi (New York: MLA, 1992). See both the "Suggestions for Further Reading" within the text of some essays and the Works Cited. Of particular relevance are the bibliographies compiled by Jonathan Culler on literary theory, by Naomi Schor on feminist and gender studies, by Paula Gunn Allen on "border" studies (the intersection of gender and color), and by David Bathrick on cultural studies. Also see individual author volumes in Garland Bibliographies of Modern Critics and Critical Schools, a series initiated in 1983 as part of Garland Reference Library of the Humanities, containing annotated primary and secondary bibliographies including translations, newspaper and periodical articles, and reviews.

M11. *The Oxford Classical Dictionary.* Ed. N. G. L. Hammond and H. H. Scullard. 2nd ed. Oxford: Clarendon, 1970.

The *OCD* is a fairly recondite reference tool, featuring signed scholarly articles (many of which are extensive surveys rather than capsule summaries) and concise appended bibliographies. Although all aspects of classical civilization are covered, the emphasis is upon literature and biography. If you have little Latin and less Greek, you might wish to use the *OCD* in conjunction with the *New Century Classical Handbook* (S99).

Contents:

1. Greek and Roman civilization from Greek pre-history through the death of the Emperor Constantine in A.D.337 (with a few later entries).
2. Mythological and legendary figures and places.[1]
3. Accounts of historical peoples and persons (including leading Christians).[2]
4. Literary forms and writers; works not separately entered.[3]
5. Festivals, customs, art, etc.
6. Places of legendary, historical, and archaeological interest.
7. Bibliographies appended to many articles.[4]
8. A General Bibliography.

Arrangement:

1. Signs and Abbreviations, pp. [ix]-xii: important for references to authors and books, both ancient and modern.
2. Dictionary proper: alphabetically arranged.
3. Appendix: General Bibliography, pp. 1151-53.
4. Index of Names, etc., that are not titles of dictionary entries, pp. [1154]-73.
5. Index to initials of contributors, pp. [1174]-76.

Review Questions:

1. For which of these would you expect to find entries: Atlantis, Alexander the Great, Medical Science in Classical Greece, Greek allegory, Cleopatra, Aphrodite, Woden, Abraham?
2. Under what subject headings would you look for an account of Circe, the enchantress in *The Odyssey*?
3. Would you expect to find a detailed plot summary of Aristophanes's play *Lysistrata*?
4. Are articles in the *OCD* signed? Are bibliographies appended? Is there an index?

Research Problems:

1. How does Caesar depict himself in *De Bello Gallico* and *De Bello Civili*? Describe the style of the *Commentaries*. Who wrote the article from which you are quoting?
2. What was the tyrant Dionysius's most successful literary work? What literary relics did Dionysius possess?
3. Where was the probable location of the sanctuary in which the Lenaea was celebrated? What was the chief importance of this festival? Cite an English-language work in which the Lenaea is discussed.
4. How did Flavius Josephus save his life? What was his first literary work? Cite an English translation of his writings and three critical, nonbibliographical works in English about him.
5. Who were the philosopher Plato's parents? What career had Plato originally intended to follow? With what is the Seventh Letter attributed to Plato concerned? Who wrote the main entry on Plato?
6. Who was Spartacus? How many Roman armies did he defeat? Name three major classical authors who serve as sources for his biography.

Notes (*OCD*)

1. Also see Edward Tripp, *Crowell's Handbook of Classical Mythology* (New York: Crowell, 1970), or its paperback twin, *The*

Meridian Handbook of Classical Mythology, and *The Mythology of All Races* (S71).

2. For further coverage, see Michael Grant, *Greek & Latin Authors: 800 B.C.-A.D. 1000* (New York: Wilson, 1980); *The Encyclopedia of World Art* (S70); *The Encyclopedia of Philosophy* (S67); *The Encyclopaedia of Religion* (S68); *The New Catholic Encyclopedia* (S73); and *Encyclopaedia Judaica* (S69).
   If you are interested in the Bible as literature, you will want to become familiar with *The New Oxford Annotated Bible* (S14); *The Interpreter's Dictionary of the Bible* (S11); and Robert Alter and Frank Kermode, *The Literary Guide to the Bible* (Cambridge: Bellknap/Harvard, 1987).
3. Major literary works are entered and summarized in *The New Century Classical Handbook* (S99). Also see *The Oxford Companion to Classical Literature*, 2nd ed., ed. M. C. Howatson (Oxford: OUP, 1989); *Cassell's Encyclopedia of World Literature* (S104); *The Oxford Companion to the Theatre* (S106); *The Reader's Encyclopedia of World Drama* (S105); and *The New Princeton Encyclopedia of Poetry and Poetics* (S6).
4. For English-language criticism of classical writers, see Thomas Gwinup and Fidelia Dickinson, *Greek and Roman Authors: A Checklist of Criticism*, 2nd ed. (Metuchen, NJ: Scarecrow, 1982). For more extensive listings, see Garland's five-volume Classical World Bibliographies series (1978), which includes bibliographies on classical literature, rhetoric, history, and religion. A new third edition of *The Oxford Classical Dictionary*, edited by Simon Hornblower and Antony Spawforth, is forthcoming.

M12. *The Penguin Companion to Literature: European.* Vol. 2. Ed. Anthony Thorlby. Harmondsworth, Middlesex: Penguin, 1969.

This is the second volume of a four-volume series covering world literature, the other titles being *The Penguin Companion to Literature: Classical and Byzantine, Oriental and African*, ed. D. R. Rudley and D. M. Lang (1969); *The Penguin Companion to Literature: English and Commonwealth*, ed. David Daiches (1971); and *The Penguin Companion to American Literature*, ed. Malcolm Bradbury, Eric Mottram, and Jean Franco (1971). This last work includes the literature of Latin America.

Contents:

1. Entries primarily for literary authors with brief biographies; also some philosophers, historians, etc.
2. Fifth century A.D. to present.
3. Main works briefly described.
4. Available editions and translations.[1]
5. Selected criticism.
6. Some entries for movements, anonymous works, classes of literature (Latin hymns), anonymous writers (the Archpoet), literature of certain periods (Romanian literature before 1850), and literary types (bildungsroman).[2]

Arrangement:

1. Identification of contributors, pp. 11-15; their initials appear in brackets at the end of their articles and before the bibliography.
2. Abbreviations of titles of books and articles cited in the bibliographies.
3. Alphabetical entries; articles are followed by bibliographies in small type. If a two-paragraph bibliography, the first paragraph lists editions and translations not given in the article itself; the second lists selected criticism.
4. Cross-refererences indicated by an arrow; multiple cross-references by a double arrow.
5. Guide to Entries by Language and Country: alphabetical list by language in which the author wrote, not by country of origin. (Thus, Ionesco is listed under France, having written in French, and not under Romania where he was born.) Note that all Albanian writers are followed by all Austrian writers, etc. Within the country, listing is chronological. The listing entry also gives the author's birth and death dates and profession (if other than literature) or literary specialization.

Review Questions:

1. For which of the following would you expect to find entries: Cervantes, Solzhenitsyn, Pushkin, Virgil, Swiss-German dialect literature, expressionism, Montesquieu, French literary criticism, Whitman, Omar Khayyam, Samuel Beckett?
2. What kind of bibliographical aid is provided by the *Penguin Companions*?
3. Are authors listed alphabetically in the Guide to Entries?

Research Problems:

1. What are Marie de France's *Le Fresne* and *Lanval* about? Whose illegitimate daughter could Marie de France have been? Whose half sister? What is her importance for French literature? Name the critic you are following.
2. With what non-German modern writer has Günther Grass most often been compared? What works by this writer were published in the same year that Grass published *Die Blechtrommel*? How does the drum operate in this novel? Cite two critical works of the mid-1960s in which Grass is discussed.
3. When did Isaak Babel produce most of his work? What is the *Konarmiya* about? What are the characteristics of his style? Why is the date of his death uncertain? Cite the English translation of his stories.
4. Name the Italian novelist, born in the same year as Antonin Artaud, who wrote *The Leopard*. Describe *The Leopard*. Whose description are you quoting?
5. When did Ernst Cassirer come to America? What is his major work? When was it translated into English? Cite two secondary works discussing his philosophy.
6. What movement was founded by the Italian writer Filippo Tommaso Marinetti? What did the movement advocate? What other Italians were associated with the movement? In what other country did the movement take hold?

Notes (*Penguin*)

1. For a more extensive listing of translations, see *The Literatures of the World in English Translation* (S97), *Index Translationum* (S96), and *Yearbook of Comparative and General Literature* (S98).
2. For subjects lending themselves to a comparative literature approach, see *Bibliography of Comparative Literature* (S94), *Yearbook of Comparative and General Literature* (S98), and the *Dictionary of the History of Ideas* (S24). Useful individual language bibliographies are Uwe K. Faulhaber and Penrith B. Goff, *German Literature: An Annotated Reference Guide* (New York: Garland, 1979); Fernande Bassan, Paul F. Breed, and Donald C. Spinelli, *An Annotated Bibliography of French Language and Literature* (New York: Garland, 1976); and Syracuse University Press's series A Critical Bibliography of French Literature (1947-94). Other works with foreign coverage include the *Oxford Companions* to various foreign literatures (M1, headnote); *The Oxford Classical Dictionary* (M11); *The New Century Classical Handbook* (S99); Earl Miner, Hiroko Odagiri, and Robert E. Morrell, *The Princeton Companion to Classical Japanese Literature* (Princeton: Princeton UP, 1985); Gale's American Literature, English Literature, and World Literatures: An Information Guide Series (part of Gale's Information Guide Library); *The Bloomsbury Guide to Women's Literature*, ed. Claire Buck (New York: Prentice Hall General Reference, 1992); *Encyclopedia of Post-Colonial Literatures in English* (S102); *Reader's Encyclopedia of Eastern European Literature* (S111); the *New Princeton Encyclopedia of Poetry and Poetics* (S6); *Motif-Index of Folk Literature* (S16), Benét's *Reader's Encyclopedia* (S101); *The Oxford Companion to the Theatre* (S106); *Modern World Theater* (S107); *Reader's Encyclopedia of World Drama* (S105); *Encyclopedia of World Literature in the 20th Century* (S108); *Macmillan Guide to Modern World Literature* (S112); *World Authors 1950-1970: A Companion Volume to Twentieth-Century Authors*, ed. John Wakeman (New York: Wilson, 1975), with quinquennial supplements currently through 1990 (1995); *Biography Index* (S30); and *Chambers Biographical Dictionary* (S31).

M13. Balay, Robert. *Guide to Reference Books.* 11th ed. Chicago: American Library Association, 1996.

The ALA *Guide*, a selective annotated bibliography of reference works, allows you to be your own reference librarian. The listings of major resources are wide-ranging and generally reliable. The introductions to classes of reference works are exercises in lucidity. This is a most helpful work to consult for general reference questions.

Contents:

1. General commentary on classes of reference works.
2. Basic general and specialized reference books in all areas.
3. Machine-readable sources.
4. Works in foreign languages as well as in English.[1]
5. Coverage through 1993.
6. Full publishing information as well as description of contents, special features (e.g., indexes, bibliographies), occasional commentary on differences between new and older editions.
7. Library of Congress card number for almost all entries.

Arrangement:

1. Table of Contents, pp. vii-xv.
2. Principal abbreviations, pp. xvii-xix.
3. Basic subject divisions:
   Part A. General Reference Works.
   Part B. The Humanities.
   Part C. Social and Behavioral Sciences.
   Part D. History and Area Studies.
   Part E. Science, Technology, and Medicine.
4. Geographic headings arranged by land mass (e.g., North American, South America), then by Region (East Asia), then alphabetically by country.
5. Cross-references by code number.[2]
6. Index includes authors, editors, compilers, and some title entries.

Review Questions:

1. Which of the following would you expect to find described in the *Guide*: a German-language bibliography of music, a handbook to civil engineering, an encyclopedia of Yucatan history, a journal of Russian periodical abstracts?
2. Does Balay describe new editions of older reference works? Are reviews of the reference works located?
3. What code letter distinguishes reference works on the humanities?
4. Are titles listed in the index?

Research Problems:

1. Cite the most comprehensive collection of literary parodies in English. Is there an anthology devoted to parodies of twentieth-century American and British literature?
2. List seven standard (i.e., non-pictorial) French-English dictionaries suitable for American students. Which was reprinted in 1992?
3. Cite two English-language reference works with some bibliography on parapsychology. Which one is multivolumed?
4. What books (including supplements) by Morgan and Smith provide a bibliography of German literature in English translation between 1481 and 1960? How do the superseded and present supplements differ? To what series does Batts's bibliography belong?
5. Cite a work published in 1979 and supplemented in 1984, 1989, and 1992 that deals with American drama criticism and that updates an earlier work. (The earlier work provides coverage through 1976, including the coverage in its supplements.) Who compiled the earlier work? Who compiled a critical collection on post-1945 American playwrights?
6. Cite an encyclopedia entitled a dictionary published in the early 1970s that is concerned specifically with British folktales. How are the various tales classified?

Notes (Balay)

1. The British counterpart of the Balay *Guide* is Walford's *Guide to Reference Material* (S23), which includes more foreign and fewer

American works. Also see American Literature, English Literature, and World Literatures: An Information Guide Series, especially for descriptions of reference works on less commonly treated subjects, e.g., Asian, Black African, Indian, and West-Indian literature in English.

2. Since cross-reference entries for a single subject may be dispersed to fit the requirements of the *Guide*'s classification scheme, be sure to check the index under all the key words in your subject. Another helpful technique is to check the appropriate General Reference Works section, even if your subject is quite limited in scope.

M14. *The Dictionary of National Biography.* Ed. Sir Leslie Stephen and Sir Sidney Lee. 63 vols. 1885-1901; rpt. in 21 vols. London: Oxford University Press, 1921-22.

Vol. 22 [First] *Supplement.* 1901; rpt. London: Oxford University Press, 1959-60.

The Twentieth Century D. N. B. London: Oxford University Press, 1912-.

The *DNB* is the classic source for British biography,[1] as monumental a work in its field as the *OED* and the *New CBEL* are in theirs. The biographies are scholarly and extensive, biographies of minor figures are abundant, and the appended bibliographies are an additional useful feature.[2] If you lack the time to read a full-length "life" the *DNB* is the best substitute.

The dictionary proper (volumes 1-21) is described below in detail. Additions to the *DNB* are described only with regard to their notable differences from the original volumes.

Contents (vols. 1-21):

1. Biographies of notable British subjects and rulers, listed under their given names, from the earliest times, and now deceased: includes

early settlers in America, Britishers who gained fame abroad, and persons of foreign birth who gained fame in Britain.

2. Those who died prior to January 22, 1901 (Queen Victoria's death date), arranged in a single alphabet.
3. Legendary British figures (e.g., Robin Hood).
4. Signed articles by experts, with sources of information (often personal) cited.
5. Bibliographies (bracketed) following each article.

Arrangement:

1. List of Contributors to vols. 1-22 (note that this includes the first Supplement): 1: xi-xx.
2. Index to each volume at the end of the respective volume. Birth and death dates as well as page numbers are given.
3. Additional lives to be found in the first *Supplement* (vol. 22) are noted at the bottom of each page of each index, in the appropriate alphabetical place.

Contents and Arrangement (*Suppl.*—vol. 22):

1. Those who died prior to January 22, 1901 but were excluded from their proper place in vols. 1-21, either because they died too late (publication extended over a fifteen-year period) or because they were accidentally or deliberately omitted.
2. Arranged in its own single alphabet.
3. Its own index at end.

Contents and Arrangement (*The Twentieth-Century D.N.B.*):

1. Ten volumes to date:
   Suppl. [2]: 1901-1911 (3 vols. in a single alphabet).
   Suppl. [3]: 1912-21.
   Suppl. [4]: 1922-30.
   Suppl. [5]: 1931-40.
   Suppl. [6]: 1941-50.
   Suppl. [7]: 1951-60.
   Suppl. [8]: 1961-70.
   Suppl. [9]: 1971-80.

Suppl. [10]: 1981-85.
Suppl. [11]: 1901-90. "With an Index covering the years 1901-1990 in one alphabetical series."[3]

Review Questions:

1. John Ruskin died in 1900. In which volume of the *DNB* would you expect to find his biography? In which volume would you look for the biography of King George V (d. 1936)? Of Neville Chamberlain (d. 1940)?
2. If you don't know your subject's death date, how can you discover it by using the *DNB* indexes?
3. When is it necessary to consult *Missing Persons*?
4. For which of the following would you expect to find entries: Harold Pinter, John Harvard, Mahatma Gandhi, Florence Nightingale, Merlin, Caedmon, Joseph Lister, Benedict Arnold, John Millingon Synge, Eugene O'Neill, Virginia Woolf, Winston Churchill, T. S. Eliot?
5. Why was there a need for the first *Supplement*, which covers the same years as the main dictionary?
6. Which supplementary volume contains an index to all the twentieth-century entries?
7. How frequently will supplements be published from this time forward?

Research Problems:

1. From the *DNB* entry for Oscar Wilde, can you ascertain for what offenses Wilde was imprisoned? Do you feel that the biographer's description of *The Picture of Dorian Grey* is critically clear and fair-minded? How would you explain the limitations of the Wilde entry, and what does this suggest about the *DNB* as a whole?
2. How old was Robert Graves when he died? Was this the first time his death was reported? Explain. Who wrote the essay?
3. Who were Benjamin Disraeli's ancestors? When did the D'Israelis become British citizens?
4. Under what pen name did Elizabeth Mackintosh write? When did she die? With which English king is *The Daughter of Time* concerned? Which of her other works deal with monarchs?

5. What is the earliest work in which King Arthur is mentioned at length? Which twelfth-century work is considered worthless for historical information about Arthur? How did Arthur obtain command of the British army? According to the biographers, who seduced Guenevere? Who wrote the *DNB* article on Arthur?
6. Where did Katherine Mansfield grow up? Where did she spend most of her life after 1917? How old was she when she died? To which Russian writer has she been compared? In what work does her second husband describe their marriage?

Notes (*DNB*)

1. For biographies of Americans, see the *Dictionary of American Biography* (S26), the *Dictionary of Literary Biography* (S25), *Who's Who in America* (S29), and *Who Was Who in America* (S28). Worldwide biographical coverage is provided by *Biography Index* (S30) and *Essay and General Literature Index* (M27); *Contemporary Authors* (M16) and *Chambers Biographical Dictionary* (S31) provide capsule biographies. Since the *DNB* enters only the deceased, it may be updated with *Who's Who* (M15) and supplemented by *Who Was Who* (S27).
2. You will need to update the bibliographies, especially those of the earlier volumes.
3. The quinquennial supplements will continue. Two indexes to each are provided, one classified by occupation and one alphabetically. You will also want to consult *Corrections and Additions to the Dictionary of National Biography* (Boston: G. K. Hall, 1966), containing emendations from research published in the *Bulletin* of the Institute of Historical Research (University of London) and cumulated for *Bulletin* volumes that appeared between 1923 and 1963; and *The DNB Missing Persons: From the Beginnings to 1985*, ed. C. S. Nicholls (Oxford: OUP, 1993), containing 1,086 persons omitted from the earlier volumes.

M15. *Who's Who 1995: An Annual Biographical Dictionary.* London: A. and C. Black, 1849-.

Who's Who originated midway through the nineteenth century as a list of British nobility and government officials. In 1897, the "First year of New Issue," it became the biographical dictionary it is today. Although entries for persons of rank are retained, merit is largely the governing factor for eligibility. It is impossible to buy one's way into *Who's Who*. Reliable biographies of living British subjects make *Who's Who* a major tool for updating the *Dictionary of National Biography*. *Who's Who 1995*, published in 1995, is described below.

Contents:

1. Only living subjects.[1]
2. All fields.
3. Principally British but some entries for famous foreigners.[2]
4. Concise biographical data: occupation, birth date, names of parents and spouses, education, awards or titles, positions held, avocations, address, telephone number,[3] and club memberships; list of works with their dates for authors, list of films and plays with their dates for actors, etc.

Arrangement:

1. Abbreviations, pp. 4-30.
2. Obituary, pp. 31-36, lists names and death dates of those who died in the year before the volume went to press.
3. Entries for the British royal family, pp. 38-39.
4. Dictionary proper, alphabetically arranged, with cross-references to other family members.

Review Questions:

1. For which of the following would you expect to find entries in the most recent volume of *Who's Who*: John Fowles, Elizabeth Bowen, Vanessa Redgrave, Bill Clinton?
2. What bibliographical information is provided by *Who's Who*?

3. What personal information is provided? What guarantee of accuracy is given the reader?
4. What biographical reference work can *Who's Who* be used to update?
5. To what work are *Who's Who* entries transferred upon the deaths of their subjects?

Research Problems:

1. As of 1995, who was the Duke of Norfolk? When did a Howard first hold this title? What is the oldest title the present Duke holds?
2. When was Kenneth Branagh born? Where did he study acting? In which films did he act in 1993? At what address can he be contacted?
3. What films did Franco Zeffirelli make in the 1960s? For what is he famous aside from filmmaking? What is the title of his autobiography?
4. Give full death dates for the following: Marchette Chute, John Wain, Sam Wanamaker, and Jessica Tandy.
5. For which Musketeer films did George MacDonald Fraser write the screenplays? What role did John Hurt play in the BBC television production of *I, Claudius*?
6. Where was the poet Richard Eberhart born? How old was he in 1995? To whom did he act as tutor?

Notes (*Who's Who*)

1. Proofs are sent to subjects for yearly revision unless *Who's Who* lacks a current address for the subject. Entries for the deceased are moved to *Who Was Who* (S27).
2. Note the profusion of specialized "Who's Who's," based upon nationality, race, profession, etc. In particular, see *Who's Who in America* (S29) and *Who Was Who in America* (S28), and *Who's Who in the Theatre* (1912-), currently published by Gale.
3. The address may be that of an office rather than a personal residence, and telephone numbers are often omitted.

M16. *Contemporary Authors: A Bio-Bibliographical Guide to Current Authors and Their Works: A Bio-Bibliographical Guide to Current Writers in Fiction, General Nonfiction, Poetry, Journalism, Drama, Motion Pictures, Television, and Other Fields.* Detroit: Gale, 1962-.[1]

Contemporary Authors is international in scope, includes nonliterary authors, and is issued semiannually. Its coverage is both broad (more than 100,000 authors) and up-to-date. The incorporated bibliographies are particularly valuable for authors not yet well established.

Contents:

1. Currently published authors (other than vanity published).
2. Frequently taught authors who died since 1900.[2]
3. "Media people."
4. All fields, but not exclusively technical writers.
5. Mostly American but also foreigners whose works have been published in the United States or have been translated into English.
6. Biographies verified by the subject.[3]
7. Biographical sketches subdivided into these categories:
   a. Personal—family background, education, current address.
   b. Career—jobs, military service, membership in organizations.
   c. Writing—list of work with dates.[4]
   d. Work in Progress.
   e. Sidelights—critical appraisal of major writers based upon judicious quotation from major critics, significant statements by the author, significant events in the subject's life; some interviews.
   f. Biographical/Critical Sources—a secondary bibliography.[5]
8. Death dates of contemporary deceased authors.
9. Obituaries: the location within *CA* of obituary citations (lists of periodicals containing death notices) are incorporated into the indexes.

Arrangement:

1. Alphabetical within each volume.

2. *CA's Permanent Series*, including entries for deceased and retired writers, was discontinued in 1978, but citations to the two existing volumes are given in the index as CAP-1 and CAP-2.
3. The *Contemporary Authors* First Revision (R) and New Revision (CANR) Series update earlier entries that have changed significantly. See the *CA* index for citations to both revised series.
4. A cumulative current index to all *CA* series and some twenty-five other reference series is published as a separate paperbound volume. Within the index listing, the most recent *CA* sketch stands first; no acronym denotes the original (unrevised) *CA* series.

Review Questions:

1. For which of the following would you expect to find entries in *Contemporary Authors*: a writer who died before World War II, a writer on science, a virtually unknown writer, an academic literary critic?
2. What is the nationality of most of the writers listed?
3. Can you learn an author's death date from *Contemporary Authors*? What other necrological information can you find?
4. What kinds of bibliographical information are provided by *Contemporary Authors*?

Research Problems:

1. In what periodicals can you find death notices for the American writer Langston Hughes? Which volumes of *Contemporary Literary Criticism* (*CLC*) treat him?
2. What was Ted Hughes's first published work? To whom was he first married? Through 1961, what prizes had he won? Whose poems did he edit and co-translate with Assia Gutmann for Cape Goliard Press in 1968 (published the following year in an expanded edition by Harper)?
3. What was Brian Earnshaw writing in the first half of the 1970s? What is the title of his 1968 science-fiction novel? Where can one find reviews of his work? What is *Living with Men*? What is *The German Mania?*
4. Compare the entry for Kenneth Muir in volume 44 of the New Revision Series of *Contemporary Authors* with two earlier *CA*

entries. What new sources of information, i.e., new rubrics, do you find in the latest New Revision Series entries? Which of Muir's translations was published in 1990? Did Muir's address change in the decades between the original *CA* entry and the most recent one?

5. Where did Woody Allen go to school? Which entertainers did he write for? Name the screenplay that he wrote in 1990. Whose book about him was published in 1991?
6. Who is Larry McCaffery? Which filmmakers does he especially admire? Which periodicals contain discussions of his work?

Notes (*Contemporary Authors*)

1. Revisions began in 1967. Original volumes 1-44 have been superseded by the two ongoing series.
2. *Contemporary Authors* was initially a guide to living authors, but beginning with volume 104 authors deceased since 1900 have been included, many of them as "Brief Entries," that have been or will be expanded.
3. In the earlier volumes, the symbols +, ++, or * indicate an unverified sketch.
4. This is often not a complete bibliography; for example, contributions to periodicals are generally not specified. Because of additions to the biography, critical discussion, and bibliography, it is best to use the most recent sketch.
5. Of particular value are references, both at the end of many sketches and in the index, to *Contemporary Literary Criticism: Excerpts from Criticism of the Works of Today's Novelists, Poets, Playwrights, and Other Creative Writers*, ed. Carolyn Riley (Detroit: Gale Research, 1973-). This is a compilation of excerpts by well-known contemporary critical and creative writers on living authors and authors deceased no earlier than 1960. The *Contemporary Authors* index also includes citations to more than two dozen related Gale series, among them the *Dictionary of Literary Biography* (S25); *Twentieth-Century Literary Criticism* (1978); *Contemporary Authors Autobiography Series* (1984-); *Contemporary Authors Biographical Series*, 3 vols. (1986-89), each volume dealing respectively with American novelists, poets, and dramatists

since World War II; and *Children's Literature Review* (S90), a *CA* supplement of excerpts from reviews, criticism, and commentary on children's books. Also see Patricia Pate Havelice, *Index to Literary Biography*, 2 vols. (Metuchen: Scarecrow, 1975); and its *First Supplement*, 2 vols. (1983), especially for foreign authors; and the *Biography and Genealogy Master Index: A Consolidated Index to More than 3,200,000 Biographical Sketches in Over 350 Current and Retrospective Biographical Dictionaries*, ed. Miranda C. Herbert and Barbara McNeil, 2nd ed., 8 vols. with ongoing supplements (Detroit: Gale, 1980-), available on-line.

For related subjects, see *World Authors 1950-1970* and its supplements (M12,n.2); *Columbia Dictionary of Modern European Literature*, ed. Jean-Albert Bede and William B. Edgerton, 2nd ed. (New York: Columbia UP, 1980); *Contemporary Literary Critics* (M3,n.2); James Vinson's Contemporary Writers Series (New York: St. Martin's, 1980-82), four bibliographical volumes, all in third editions, on dramatists, novelists, and poets, respectively; and *Current Biography* (New York: Wilson, 1940-), a monthly periodical, cumulated annually, and recently made more convenient through its cumulated indexes through 1990. Gale's useful theatrical counterpart of *Contemporary Authors* for performance criticism and research is *Contemporary Theatre, Film, and Television: A Biographical Guide Featuring Performers, Directors, Writers, Producers, Designers, Managers, Choreographers, Technicians, Composers, Executives, Dancers, and Critics in the United States and Great Britain* (1984-).

GENERAL REVIEW 1

1. Who is responsible for the first collected edition of Poe's letters? When did it appear? Has it been superseded? Explain. Who discusses Poe's debt to the British quarterlies?

2. Cite three English-language guides to philosophy published in the 1980s. Which is a revision? Which is the longest? Which is written for "a diversity of users"?

3. Name five authors who frequented Will's Coffee House in London. What club met at London's Mermaid Tavern?

4. In which of P. G. Wodehouse's works is the adjective "goofy" first found? (Cite date, chapter, and page.) Whom is the Hugo award named after? When were Hugos first presented?

5. On what writer does the American professor Marvin Magalaner primarily publish? Where was Magalaner educated, and how many children does he have? To what modern literary encyclopedia has Huntington Brown, retired American professor, contributed? Where has he taught? What are his feelings about American education?

6. Name eleven Caroline dramatists. Which three seem to be the best? Whose critical opinions are you following?

7. Cite one short story and three novels in which vigilantes play a part. Which of the authors of these works was a Californian by

birth? Which of his novels won a Pultizer prize? Who won the Pulitzer drama award in 1940?

8. What was written in 1964 about the British playwright John Osborne? When did Osborne first attain sufficient fame to receive critical attention? By considering the number of Osborne entries for 1970, determine whether the dramatist's reputation had grown or declined by the end of the decade. Cite the names of the books or journals in which the 1970 critical works on Osborne appeared. (Explain all title abbreviations.)

9. Approximately how many plays did Eugène Labiche have a hand in? Supply the English titles of two of his most famous farces. Which social classes does Labiche satirize? Which stock characters and situations does he employ? Name a famous German composer-poet born two years before Labiche. Name a famous Russian novelist born three years after Labiche.

10. What key word in many of the works of colonial American poet Anne Bradstreet points to one of her chief thematic concerns? Name a graduate of Harvard College who also wrote private meditational poetry. Which book of Bradstreet's did he own?

11. What were "patent theatres"? When were the patents finally revoked?

12. What professions are currently practiced by Naguib Mahfouz, Anna Russell, and Nicholas William Shakespeare?

13. What were the first works printed and etched by William Blake?

14. Who were the two most important formulators of modern theories of the grotesque? Who applied Bahktinian principles of the grotesque to elucidate the way in which Augustan poets searched for elevated discourse?

15. In what literary sources is Minos depicted as a king associated with Zeus, as ruling the dead, and as married to Pasiphae, the daughter of Helios? (Explain all abbreviations and cite exact references to the sources.)

16. How long did it take Handel to write the *Messiah*? What is Ralph Vaughan Williams's best-known piece of incidental music to a Greek play?

17. Where was Jean Toomer educated? With whom was he ranked as a Harlem Renaissance writer? Which of his works is considered his best? To what does S. P. Fullwinder attribute Toomer's loss of creativity?

18. With what episodes does Finland's national epic, the *Kalevala*, begin and end? What is "the Sampo"? Describe the traditional meter of old Finnish folk poetry. What American poem was partly inspired by a German translation of the *Kalevala*? Whose English prose translation of the *Kalevala* appeared in 1963?

19. Cite a work published in 1983 on folk drama as a source of Native American theater.

20. What are the real names of British writers Michael Innes and Frank O'Connor? What pseudonyms were used by Cicily Isabel Andrews and Eric Arthur Blair? What was each writer's earliest work?

21. Which American president first used the term "muckraking"? What literary work was the source of the term? Whose autobiography includes a history of the movement? List four collections of the autobiographer's articles.

22. Name two atlases of British history published no earlier than the 1980s. Which includes maps of England's overseas possessions?

23. What is the source of the phrase "angry young men"? Which American writers can be considered within the apocalyptic tradition?

24. Define the Husserlian term *Lebenswelt*. Why do critics of the early Geneva School place an author's personal papers "off-limits"? In the 1970s, who wrote a useful work on phenomenology and literature?

25. Whose cousin was Lady Jane Grey, later wife of Guildford Dudley? Who was her tutor? At whose funeral was she chief mourner? Who vouched for her proficiency in Greek? What were her last acts? What is the leading authority for the events of Lady Jane's nine-days' reign?

26. Quote, in modern English, the *Feoh* section of the English *Runic Poem.* What is the earliest extant text? Whose edition was published in 1915? In what collection?

27. What do we know about the number of slaves in classical Greece and Rome?

28. With which Catholic Feast day are mystery plays associated? Who ruled England in the year the feast was first declared? Who ruled in the year the feast was first observed as a holy day? What scholarly work on the mysteries was published in 1966?

29. What five-volume scientific publication has the Honorable Miriam Rothschild authored? How many journal articles has she written? What are the favorite recreations of Wolf Mankowitz and Harold Pinter?

30. Juliet's father speaks of Romeo as a "portly youth"; Hal tells Falstaff to "Come out of that fat room." What did "portly" and "fat" mean to Shakespeare? When did these works assume their modern meanings?

31. Who were the originators of New York's gay drama? Whose play appealed to mainstream audiences? Whose play parodies Marlowe's *Tamburlaine*? Who wrote the essay you are reading?

32. What are the most important sources for a biography of Edith Wharton? Who used the Wharton manuscripts at Yale for the definitive biography? Whose work explores the friendship between Edith Wharton and Henry James?

CHAPTER 3

BIBLIOGRAPHIES

Bibliographies of Bibliographies:

M17. *A World Bibliography of Bibliographies*

M18. *Bibliographic Index*

Current Bibliographies:

M19. Specialized Bibliographies in Scholarly Journals

M20. Checklists: *Twentieth-Century Short Story Explication*

M21. *Bibliography of American Literature*

M22. *National Union Catalog: Pre-1956 Imprints*

M22. *National Union Catalog: 1956-*

Retrospective Bibliographies:

M23. *Short-Title Catalogue*

M24. *American Bibliography*

M17. Besterman, Theodore. *A World Bibliography of Bibliographies and of Bibliographical Catalogues, Calendars, Abstracts, Digests, Indexes, and the Like.* 4th ed. Revised and Greatly Enlarged Throughout. 5 vols. Lausanne: Societas Bibliographica, 1965-66.

Toomey, Alice F. *A World Bibliography of Bibliographies 1964-1974: A List of Works Represented by Library of Congress Printed Catalog Cards, A Decennial Supplement to Theodore Besterman, A World Bibliography of Bibliographies.* 2 vols. Totowa, NJ: Rowman and Littlefield, 1977.

Besterman, the most complete multi-volumed list of bibliographies, is international in scope and arranged by subject. It is a valuable source for retrospective book lists not subject to revision. For example, the question "What English translations of classical authors were available prior to the nineteenth century?" is answered by the entry for Lewis William Brüggeman's *A View of the English Editions, Translations and Illustrations of the Ancient Greek and Latin Authors*, published in 1797, and found under the heading Classical Literature—Translations, English. For bibliographies of literary authors, Besterman's chief virtue lies in its convenience as a cumulated, finite work. Nevertheless, its usefulness is limited by the exclusion of all bibliographies not separately published and by the inevitable obsolescence of many entries in a non-continuous reference work of this nature. Coverage is continued through 1974 in Alice Toomey's supplement, which you should consult in conjunction with Besterman's *World Bibliography.* (The great bibliographer died in 1976.) In addition, you can supplement Besterman with the *Bibliographic Index* (M18), Nilon's *Bibliography of Bibliographies in American Literature* (S33), and Howard-Hill's *Bibliography of British Literary Bibliographies* (S32).

Contents (Besterman):

1. From the earliest bibliographies (1470) through 1963, with some later entries.
2. Only bibliographies separately published (i.e., with separate pagination) and arranged according to some permanent principle (thus excluding publishers' and general libraries' catalogs); excluded also are bibliographies in journals).[1]

3. Both primary and secondary bibliographies.
4. Limited and privately printed editions.
5. All subjects, European languages.[2]
6. Short title entries.
7. Some annotation: pagination, number of items in each bibliography (set out in square brackets), number of copies printed if a small edition, indication of private printing, explanation of ambiguous or inaccurate titles, clarification of works in series, etc.[3]

Arrangement:

1. A list of subject headings for subjects classified by countries, Vol. 1, Introduction, pp. 41-42.
2. A list of subheadings under a country classified by subjects, Vol. 1, Introduction, pp. 43-44.
3. Bibliography proper: arranged alphabetically by subject; subject headings usually quite broad.
4. Within the subject heading or subheading, chronologically by date of publication.
5. Extensive cross-references.
6. Index: Vol. 5[4] includes in one alphabet authors, editors, translators, titles of anonymous and serial bibliographies, libraries, archives, and patents.

Contents and Arrangement (Toomey):

1. Coverage from 1964 to 1974.
2. Entry format: copies of Library of Congress cards; additional information for some entries.
3. Subject headings generally based on the eighth edition of *LC Subject Headings*.
4. Two special arrangements (see p. xii for explanation of subdivisions within these headings):
   a. A new heading—Dissertations, Academic—including bibliographic theses and reports as well as dissertations, replaces Besterman's heading academic Writings.
   b. General bibliographies, catalogs, and indexes of periodicals are here entered under the heading Periodical Publications.

5. Continuous pagination through the two volumes.

Review Questions:

1. Is Besterman limited to bibliographies of literary subjects?
2. For which of the following would you expect to find entries:
   a. a bibliography appended to a dissertation on Keats?
   b. a bibliography pamphlet on theatrical and literary British journals, published as part of a series?
   c. a calendar (list of manuscripts) of the Byron holdings in the University of Texas library?
   d. a separately published bibliography on Browning that appeared in 1966?
   e. a French-language bibliography of ancient and modern authors, published in 1704?
   f. a bibliography of Jane Austen's letters? A critical bibliography of Jane Austen?
3. How can you determine the extent of the bibliographies entered?
4. What indication of availability does Besterman provide?
5. What principles of arrangement does Besterman follow for subject entries? Within the subject heading?
6. Would you find Goethe cited in the Index? Satan? Besterman?

Research Problems:

1. What separately published bibliography was compiled by the critic, poet, and novelist Allen Tate? For what bibliography did Tate serve as adviser?
2. Cite a twentieth-century catalog of the Robin Hood holdings of the public libraries in Nottingham. How many works are entered? Cite a more recent general bibliography of Robin Hood. How extensive is this work?
3. Cite an English-language bibliography of English literature translated into Hungarian. Cite an English-language bibliography of Hungarian literature translated into English.
4. Cite a bibliography of English bibles printed between 1526 and 1776. In what libraries can one find copies of the original editions of this bibliography containing manuscript notes and additions?

5. Cite a bibliography published in 1965 of Masters' theses on all subjects. Cite a 1971 bibliography of theses written by non-British authors and held by British libraries. Cite a bibliography published in 1955 of Masters' and doctoral theses about the literature of the American South.
6. What separately published bibliographies (including editions and appreciations) had Jacob Blanck compiled prior to 1964? Have any of these been reprinted?

Notes (Besterman)

1. See William A. Wortman, ed., *A Guide to Serial Bibliographies for Modern Literature*, 2nd. ed. (New York: MLA, 1995). Note that not only are regularly published bibliographies in serials excluded, but so too are bibliographies appended to book-length critical studies or to critical studies in periodicals.
2. Works in, though not on, Oriental languages are excluded. Works in Eastern European languages are minimally represented.
3. London and Paris are understood as the places of publication for English and French works, respectively, if no other place is cited.
4. Note that pagination is continuous through all five volumes.

M18. *Bibliographic Index: A Cumulative Bibliography of Bibliographies*. New York: Wilson, 1938-.

Bibliographic Index is a universal subject listing of bibliographies published separately and, unlike Besterman (M17), of bibliographies *included* in books and in periodical articles. Currently published biannually and cumulated annually,[1] *BI* both supplements and updates Besterman. Its major value for students of literature is as a current index to bibliographies of British, American, and essentially Western European authors.[2] Since most literary authors are treated as subjects, *BI*'s subject classification presents little difficulty. On-line computer searching is available.

Contents:

1. Bibliographies: those published separately.
2. Those appearing as parts of books, pamphlets, and periodicals. Excludes dissertations.
3. Chiefly indexes works in the Roman alphabet.
4. Literary subjects generally limited to author (rather than title) entries; only anonymous works receive separate citations.
5. Literary genres and movements found under the appropriate subject headings.
6. Only extensive bibliographies cited: fifty or more titles.[3]
7. Unannotated.[4]

Arrangement:

1. Keys to general abbreviations and periodicals.
2. Index proper: broad subject headings and subject subdivisions arranged alphabetically.[5]
3. Within the subject heading, bibliographies listed alphabetically by author.[6]
4. Within the literary author heading, both primary ("by") and secondary ("about") bibliographies.
5. Cross-references:
   a. from pseudonyms to entry name.
   b. from subjects to related topics, e.g., "Comedy," See also "Tragicomedy."[7]

Review Questions:

1. Is the *BI* limited to bibliographies on English and American literature?
2. Are the listed bibliographies annotated by the editors of *BI*?
3. To locate a book-length study in English of a major literary figure—a study containing an extensive, annotated bibliography—would *BI* or the *MLA International Bibliography* be the more useful tool? Why?
4. For which of the following might you expect to find entries:
   a. a bibliographical treatment of exorcism, published in a popular general interest magazine?

b. bibliographies on the anonymous *Song of Roland*?
c. a scholarly bibliography in a pamphlet on Bertolt Brecht?
d. a bibliography on romanticism in art, published in a periodical?
e. a bibliographic essay written in French about T. S. Eliot?

Research Problems:

1. Locate a bibliography published in 1993 on Mexican-American authors. How many pages long is it? Is it annotated?
2. Cite a work published in an expanded edition by Oxford University Press in 1989 that contains an annotated bibliography of writings by American prisoners. Cite a work published in 1974 containing a bibliography of works dealing with the depiction of prisons in Elizabethan literature. Give volume and page numbers for the bibliography.
3. Find a bibliography of works about the American poet, critic, and scholar John Berryman, published late in the 1960s. Cite full publishing information. Is this work devoted exclusively to bibliography, or is the bibliography only a small part of the work? When was Berryman born?
4. Cite a book published by Fairleigh Dickinson University Press in 1972 that contains a brief bibliography of works dealing with Jews in literature. Under what *Bibliographic Index* subject heading did you find this title? Under what other headings would you be likely to find bibliographies on this subject?
5. Cite a 1951 literary study with a bibliography of the self-proclaimed descendant and namesake of Lord Byron, who styled himself Major Byron. How extensive is the work's bibliography? Is it annotated?
6. Using the volumes of *Bibliographic Index* issued in the 1970s, compile a list of primary and/or secondary bibliographies on the Swedish film director Ingmar Bergman. What conclusions can you draw about the recency of *BI* coverage?

Notes (*BI*)

1. Permanent volumes containing bibliographies published between 1939 and 1968 are cumulated in periods varying between two and six years.
2. Also see Howard-Hill's *Bibliography of British Literary Bibliographies* (S32); Nilon's *Bibliography of Bibliographies in American Literature* (S33); and *Bulletin of Bibliography* (Westport, CT: Greenwood, 1897-), a quarterly journal.
3. "Exceptions are made for bibliographies of works by or about a person, or for specialized or topical material, which may be listed with fewer citations" (Prefatory note).
4. But annotation within the bibliography listed is indicated by the abbreviation "annot." Among other features, such annotation makes *Bibliographic Index* more useful as a guide to bibliographies than the *MLA International Bibliography* (M7), since the latter does not indicate annotation.
5. Subdivision headings, which follow Library of Congress classifications, are more specific than those in Besterman.
6. Prior to 1955, bibliographies were listed alphabetically by title.
7. References to related subjects and to subheadings should be carefully examined. See the Prefatory Note at the front of each volume for sample entries interpreting *Bibliographic Index* entry style.

M19. Specialized Bibliographies in Scholarly Journals

Many scholarly journals regularly include a bibliography of current works on a particular subject, often the subject to which the journal is devoted. The advantages of such specialized bibliographies over the *MLA International Bibliography* (M7) are these:

1. Specialized journals may be more current.
2. Some publish annotated bibliographies.
3. Some specialized serial bibliographies (i.e., bibliographies appearing within journals) may be more comprehensive than the *MLA* listings; others are evaluative and selective, citing only important titles published that year.

4. Serial bibliographies covering a period of years are often collected and published in book form for the researcher's convenience.

Below are a number of scholarly journals, the titles of their bibliographies, and relevant information. All the serial bibliographies listed here can be supplemented by the evaluative bibliographical essays in *The Year's Work in English Studies* (S42). For additional bibliographies, see *A Guide to Serial Bibliographies for Modern Literatures* (M17,n.1):

M19a. *Studies in English Literature 1500-1900*: "Recent Studies in the English Renaissance" [1961-, winter issues];[1] "Recent Studies in Elizabethan and Jacobean Drama" [spring issues]; "Recent Studies in the Restoration and Eighteenth Century" [summer issues];[2] "Recent Studies in the Nineteenth Century" [autumn issues]. Together these annual evaluative bibliographical essays survey the year's scholarship on literature of the sixteenth through nineteenth centuries. Note, however, that the *SEL* bibliographies now discuss only books, not articles.

M19b. *Shakespeare Quarterly*: "Shakespeare: Annotated World Bibliography" [1949-]. Appears annually. Classified (see Arrangement of Contents) and comprehensive with regard to scholarly studies; records books, dissertations, articles, and reviews of books and theatrical productions directly related to Shakespeare. Brief descriptions of contents or statements of theme for all articles and some books. An ongoing cumulation, in print and accessible by database, is in progress.

M19c. *Shakespeare Survey*: "The Year's Contributions to Shakespearian Study" [1948-]. Annual evaluative bibliographic essays. Division into three categories: Critical Studies; Shakespeare's Life, Times, and Stage; Editions and Textual Studies.

M19d. *Keats-Shelley Journal: A Periodical Devoted to Keats, Shelley, Byron, Hunt and Their Circles*: "Current Bibliography" [1950]. An annual, classified, descriptive bibliography.[3] Brief annotations for some works. Works concerning English romanticism in general are followed by those treating individual authors.[4]

Index to the bibliography includes primary authors, titles, and critics, and refers to item, not page numbers.

M19e. *Victorian Studies*: "Victorian Bibliography" [1958-].[5] Appears annually. Minimally annotated bibliography of books, dissertations, articles, and reviews. Broad classified coverage includes the arts, social sciences, science, religion, etc.[6]

M19f. *Journal of Modern Literature*: "Annual Review" [1971-]. The "Annual Review," a double issue, is a bibliography of scholarly and critical works in English, covering world literature from 1900 to the present, although the main emphasis is generally on the modernist period (1885-1950).[7] Partially annotated, i.e., while there are no citations for notes, explications, or reviews, book annotations are actually mini-reviews of half a page to a page, a useful feature; not all books are reviewed, however. Rubrics include Reference and Bibliography; Literary History; Themes and Movements; Regional, National, and Ethnic Literatures; Comparative Studies; criticism of various genres including film; and studies of individual writers. Authors and critics in a single index at back.

Review Questions:

1. In what ways are specialized journal bibliographies unlike the *MLA International Bibliography*?
2. Which journals carry bibliographies devoted to or including American literature?
3. Where can you find annual evaluative surveys of criticism dealing with American literature?
4. Which journals contain an annual bibliography of Renaissance studies? Of Shakespeare? Of Victorian literature?
5. Where can you find bibliographies of the Restoration and eighteenth century?
6. Which annual bibliographies have been collected and printed in book form?

Research Problems:

1. Using a 1995 bibliographic essay, discover what anthology marked the "official" emergence of Queer Studies into Renaissance Studies? Who is the reviewer, and whose contributions to the volume does he regard most highly?
2. Using a specialized serial bibliography that appeared in the first half of the 1980s, locate a periodical *issue* of which half is devoted to the twentieth-century Argentine writer Julio Cortázar.
3. State the full title and thesis of Caroline Franklin's 1990 essay on Byron and "the woman question." In what journal did the article appear?
4. Using an evaluative specialized serial bibliography, determine which of Shakespeare's history plays received the most critical attention in 1993. What does David Lindley find lacking in Antony Brennan's *New Critical Introduction* to the play?
5. Using a specialized serial bibliography, discover the thesis of J. L. Kendall's "A Neglected Theme in Tennyson's *In Memoriam*" (1961). Give full publication data for this article.
6. List articles that appeared in 1978 on the then forthcoming BBC-TV productions of Shakespeare's plays. (Exclude reviews of later productions.) Explain periodical abbreviations.

Notes (Spec. Biblio.)

1. Bracketed dates refer to the year in which bibliographical coverage begins; this date may not necessarily coincide with the founding of the periodical.
2. The major bibliography for this period was published for nearly half a century in *Philological Quarterly*: "The Eighteenth Century: A Current Bibliography Incorporating English Literature 1660-1800" [1926-1975]. Bibliographies for 1925-1970 are collected in *English Literature, 1660-1800: A Bibliography of Modern Studies Founded by Ronald S. Crane*, 6 vols. (Princeton: Princeton UP, 1950-72). Bibliographies since 1975 are published as separate annual volumes under the title *The Eighteenth Century: A Current Bibliography* (New York: AMS, 1978-). This is an excellent annotated interdisciplinary bibliography of English, American, and

European literature, art, history, religion, science, etc. Unfortunately, coverage is more than five years behind.

3. For cumulations, see David Bonnell Green and Edwin Graves Wilson, eds., *Keats, Shelley, Byron, Hunt and Their Circles: A Bibliography: July 1, 1950-June 30, 1962* (Lincoln: U of Nebraska P, 1964); and Robert A. Hartley, ed., *Keats, Shelley, Byron, Hunt, and Their Circles: A Bibliography: July 1, 1962-December 31, 1974* (Lincoln: U of Nebraska P, 1978).
4. Beginning with the 1984 bibliography, Hazlitt is included. The Keats-Shelley bibliography can be supplemented for other authors by *The Romantic Movement: A Selective and Critical Bibliography* [1937-], originally published in *ELH: A Journal of English Literary History* (1937-49), in *Philological Quarterly* (1950-64), in *English Language Notes* (1965-79), and since 1979 in separate annual volumes under the editorship of David V. Erdman. *The Romantic Movement* is an annual, selective, classified bibliography of romanticism in England and on the continent. Major division is by nationality. Annotations of books, articles, and reviews are descriptive and sometimes critical. Additional critical reviews are located. For collected bibliographies, see *The Romantic Movement Bibliography 1936-1970*, ed. A. C. Elkins, Jr. and L. J. Forstner, 7 vols. (Ann Arbor: Pierian, 1973).
5. During 1933-57, "Victorian Bibliography" appeared annually in *Modern Philology*.
6. Bibliographies for 1932-84 are collected in *Bibliographies of Studies in Victorian Literature*, 5 vols. (Urbana: U of Illinois P, 1945-67; New York: AMS, 1981-91). [Vol. 1 collecting studies for 1932-44, ed. William D. Templeman; vol. 2, 1945-54, ed. Austin Wright; vol. 3, 1955-64, ed Robert C. Slack]; vol. 4, 1965-74, ed. Ronald E. Freeman; vol. 5, 1975-84, ed. Richard C. Tobias.
7. Also see *Twentieth Century Literature*'s "Current Bibliography" [1954-81], quarterly annotated bibliographies of critical articles in American and foreign periodicals on world literature of the twentieth century. For an expanded cumulation, see David E. Pownall, *Articles on Twentieth Century Literature: An Annotated Bibliography 1954 to 1970*, 7 vols. (New York: Kraus-Thomson, 1973-80). *American Literature*'s "A Selected, Annotated List of Current Articles on American Literature" (1929-1990), minimally

annotated, classified checklists are cumulated in Lewis Leary's *Articles on American Literature 1900-1950* and its supplements through 1975 (S40). For full annotation, see the ongoing *American Literary Scholarship* (S34).

M20. Checklists

Walker, Warren S. *Twentieth-Century Short Story Explication: Interpretations, 1900-1975 of Short Fiction Since 1800*. 3rd ed. Hamden CT: Shoe String, 1977. [Five supplements and Volume 1 of a *New Series* covering 1989-90.]

Walker, Warren S., and Barbara K. Walker. *Twentieth-Century Short Story Explication: An Index to the Third Edition and Its Five Supplements, 1961-91* (Hamden, CT: Shoe String, 1992).

Walker's *Twentieth-Century Short Story Explication* is one example of a checklist: the simplest and shortest form of a bibliography. Often selective rather than comprehensive, and usually unannotated, a checklist may be devoted to a single work, e.g., Samuel A. Tannenbaum, *Shakespeare's "King Lear": A Concise Bibliography* (New York: Tannenbaum, 1940); to a single author, listing works by and/or about him, e.g., *The Merrill Checklist of Nathaniel Hawthorne*, comp. C. E. Prazer Clark, Jr. (Columbus, OH: Merrill, 1970); or to a broad subject, e.g., *Tudor and Stuart Drama*, comp. Irving Ribner and Clifford C. Huffman, 2nd ed. (Arlington Heights, IL: AHM, 1978).[1] *Magill's Bibliography of Literary Criticism* (see n.1), a four-volume index entitled a bibliography, which provides the same kind of information as a checklist, suggests how tenuous any refinement of classification may become.

Walker's *Twentieth-Century Short Story Explication, Supplements* I-V, and *New Series, Volume I, 1989-90* are described below:[2]

Contents:

1. Stories by writers of all nationalities.
2. Treats stories of not more than 150 pages.

3. Only explicatory criticisms: excludes source, biographical, and background studies, although particular explicatory passages from such works are cited.
4. Criticisms primarily in English.

Arrangement:

1. Alphabetical by author; within the author entry, alphabetical by title; within the title entry, alphabetical by critic.
2. A Checklist of Books used containing full title and publication data for sources. Periodical information is given as part of the individual entries, but each *Supplement* also contains a Checklist of Journals used, which is helpful for unfamiliar abbreviations.
3. Index of Short Story Writers treated.[3]

Review Questions:

1. How does a checklist differ from such standard bibliographies as the *New CBEL* or the *LHUS: Bibliography*?
2. What would you suppose is the main advantage of a checklist?
3. What kinds of criticism are not included in *Twentieth-Century Short Story Explication*?

Research Problems:

1. Which of William Carlos Williams's stories is discussed in Brooks, Purser, and Warren's *Approach to Literature*? Give full publishing information for the anthology.
2. Cite five critical pieces listed in the 1992 index on Katherine Mansfield's "A Dill Pickle." Which is the most recent?
3. Find critical articles by Norman H. Holland, Carol Cantrell, and Mark M. Anderson on Kafka's "Metamorphosis."
4. Which two of Gogol's stories received the most critical attention in 1989 and 1990?
5. Cite five explicatory discussions published prior to 1991 of Nadine Gordimer's "The Train from Rhodesia." (Supply full titles for journals and publication information for books.) Where was Gullason's essay reprinted?
6. Cite an essay by André Gide on his "Pastoral Symphony."

Notes (Checklists)

1. Some particularly useful checklists are listed below:

Adelman, Irving, and Rita Dworkin. *The Contemporary Novel: A Checklist of Critical Literature on the English Language Novel Since 1945*. 2nd ed. Lanham, MD: Scarecrow, 1996.

Alexander, Harriet Semmes, comp. *American and British Poetry: A Guide to the Criticism 1925-1978*. Athens, OH: Swallow, 1984-.

Bell, Inglis F., and Donald Baird. *The English Novel, 1578-1956: A Checklist of Twentieth-Century Criticism*. Rev. ed. Hamden, CT: Shoe String, 1974. (Continued in Palmer and Dyson below.)

Breed, Paul F., and Florence M. Sniderman, eds. *Dramatic Criticism Index: A Bibliography of Commentaries on Playwrights from Ibsen to the Avant-Garde*. Detroit: Gale, 1972.

Carpenter, Charles A. *Modern Drama Scholarship and Criticism 1966-1980: An International Bibliography*. Toronto: U of Toronto P, 1986.

Coleman, Arthur, and Gary R. Tyler. *Drama Criticism: A Checklist of Interpretations Since 1940 of English and American Plays*. 2 vols. Denver [later Chicago]: Swallow, 1966, 1971.

Eddleman, Floyd Eugene. *American Drama Criticism: Interpretations 1890-1977*. 2nd ed. Hamden: Shoe String, 1979. 1996 supplement covers criticism through 1994.

Fairbanks, Carol, and Eugene A. Engeldinger. *Black American Fiction: A Bibliography*. Metuchen, NJ: Scarecrow, 1978.

Gerstenberger, Donna, and George Hendrick. *The American Novel, 1789-1959: A Checklist of Twentieth-Century Criticism*. Denver: Swallow, 1961. Vol. 2: *Criticism Written 1960-1968*. Denver: Swallow, 1970.

Kearney, E. I., and L. S. Fitzgerald. *The Continental Novel: A Checklist of Criticism in English, 1900-1966*. Metuchen, NJ: Scarecrow, 1968. A supplement covering 1967-1980 appeared in 1983.

Kuntz, Joseph M., and Nancy C. Martinez. *Poetry Explication: A Checklist of Interpretations since 1925 of British and American Poems Past and Present*. 3rd ed. Boston: Hall,

1980. For updating, see Hall's *Guide to American Poetry Expli cation* (1989) and *Guide to British Poetry Explication* (1991-).
Magill, Frank N., ed. *Magill's Bibliography of Literary Criticism: Selected Sources for the Study of More Than 2,500 Outstanding Works of Western Literature.* 4 vols. Englewood Cliffs, NJ: Salem, 1979.
Palmer, Helen H., and Anne J. Dyson. *English Novel Explication: Criticism to 1972.* Hamden, CT: Shoe String, 1973. Ongoing supplements.
Schleuter, Paul, and June Schlueter. *English Novel: Twentieth Century Criticism.* Vol. 2. Athens: Ohio UP (Swallow), 1982. Not limited to explication.

An example of a checklist based on a particular approach is Chris Bullock and David Peck, *Guide to Marxist Literary Criticism* (Bloomington: Indiana UP, 1980). Also see the Garland and G. K. Hall series of selective bibliographies on English and American literature and literature-related subjects.

2. For more recent criticism, see the checklists of explications published annually in *The Explicator*, a journal of short criticisms. For biographical information and critical excerpts, see *Short Story Criticism* (Detroit: Gale, 1988-), an ongoing series with a cumulative index in the most recent volume.
3. Be sure to consult the cumulative index volume for all authors.

M21. Blanck, Jacob, comp. *Bibliography of American Literature.* 8 vols. New Haven: Yale University Press, 1955-89. [Vol. 8 edited and completed by Michael Winship.]

The *BAL* is the definitive American *descriptive* bibliography. That is, Blanck not only provides standard bibliographical data but also notes the physical characteristics of the earliest editions and published revisions of his entries. Though selective,[1] Blanck lists more authors than does the *LHUS: Bibliography* (M6). The latter work, however, is the standard source for important secondary bibliographies of authors and for the context of American literature.

Contents:

1. Selected authors significant in the history of American literature from the Revolution on, excluding those who died after 1930 and those who primarily wrote juvenilia.
2. All first editions of the author's works.
3. Any book or pamphlet, etc. (excluding periodical or newspaper publications) containing the first appearance of any prose (except letters) by the author.
4. Variant issues or states of the first edition.[2]
5. Illustrations, maps, binding.
6. European editions in English that preceded the American edition.
7. Reprints that might be confused with first editions or with editions containing important textual changes.
8. Sheet music.
9. Some off-[literary] subject books.
10. List of bibliographical, biographical, and critical works about the author ("Reference").
11. Locates works examined, although not a census.[3]

Arrangement:

1. Location symbols at front of each volume.
2. Alphabetical by author.
3. Within the author entry, chronological by date of publication.
4. List of secondary sources at end of each author entry.
5. Initials, Pseudonyms, and Anonyms at end of each volume.[4]

Review Questions:

1. What outstanding feature of the *BAL* distinguishes it from other general bibliographies of American literature?
2. Would you expect to find an entry for William Faulkner? For the colonial poet Anne Bradstreet? For Ralph Waldo Emerson?
3. Does the *BAL* note the first publication of a work that originally appeared in an anthology? In a magazine?
4. Would you find entries citing European editions of American works?
5. Can the *BAL* be used for finding secondary source material?

Research Problems:

1. When was Crane's *Maggie: A Girl of the Streets* originally published? What pseudonym did Crane use? When was the revised edition of *Maggie* published? Note two ways in which, by examining the title pages with regard to publisher's name and publication date, the first edition of *Maggie* can be distinguished from the revised edition.
2. What was William Dean Howells's first publication? When, where, and in what format was it published? At what library can it be seen?
3. List the complete literary works (with dates) of William Hill Brown, considered the first American novelist. Mention one modern bio-biographical study of Brown.
4. Under what title did Francis Scott Key's "The Star Spangled Banner" first appear? When and where was its earliest dated printing? Cite an essay tracing the history of its melody.
5. Explain the pagination indicated by <1-ii>, <1>-<x>, <1>-128. What is a binder's title?
6. How old was Amy Lowell when she published her first work? Who were her collaborators? How many copies were printed? When was her work first anthologized? Who was the editor? Where had the anthologized poems been published originally?

Notes (*BAL*)

1. The University of Pittsburgh's Pittsburgh Series in Bibliography, which specializes in descriptive bibliographies, complements the *BAL*. Such figures as Berryman, Hart Crane, Fitzgerald, Hawthorne, Lardner, Marianne Moore, O'Neill, and Stevens have been treated.
2. An issue consists of copies of a printing altered after initial publication. A state consists of those copies altered prior to publication or sale. See Blanck's Preface for a discussion of these terms and for an explanation of his entry form. Incidentally, the Preface to the *BAL* can serve as a pleasant capsule introduction to descriptive bibliography. If you like this subject, try William Proctor Williams and Craig S. Abbott, *An Introduction to Biblio-*

graphical and Textual Studies, 2nd ed. (New York: MLA, 1989). A literary census is a comprehensive listing, locating *all* examples of a particular class. See, for example, the *Library of Congress National Union Catalog of Manuscript Collections* (Washington: Library of Congress, 1962-); Seymour de Ricci, *Census of Medieval and Renaissance Manuscripts in the United States and Canada*, 3 vols. (1934-40), with C. U. Faye and W. H. Bond's *Supplement* (1962); and the near-census, *American Literary Manuscripts: A Checklist of Holdings in Academic, Historical, and Public Libraries, Museums, and Authors' Homes in the United States*, ed. J. Albert Robbins, 2nd ed. (Athens, GA: U of Georgia P, 1977).

Blanck attempted personally to examine all the works entered in order to minimize "ghosts." When he was unable to do so, the source is cited.

3. A census attempts to locate *all* copies.
4. See Winship's *Bibliography of American Literature: A Selective Index* (Golden, CO: North American Press, 1995).

M22. *The National Union Catalog. Pre-1956 Imprints: A Cumulative Author List Representing Library of Congress Printed Cards and Titles Reported by Other American Libraries*. 685 vols. London: Mansell, 1968-80. [Plus 68 supplementary volumes.]

The National Union Catalog: A Cumulative Author List Representing Library of Congress Printed Cards and Titles Reported by Other American Libraries. Washington: Library of Congress, 1956-. (This is the ongoing continuation of our national union catalog, appearing monthly with quarterly, annual, and quinquennial cumulations.)

A national union catalog is a listing of publications held by a nation's major library (in America, the Library of Congress)[1] and by important research libraries throughout that country. Because of its comprehensiveness, the accuracy of its entries, and the extensive descriptions of the works entered, our national union catalog is a valuable research tool for verification of bibliographical data and for locating hard-to-find publications.The current U.S. national catalog is an outgrowth of the old "LC Catalog," basically an author list of publications held by the Library of Congress up through 1942.[2] Although supplements to the "LC Catalog" were issued regularly, it was not until 1956 that those books not in the Library of Congress collection but held by other American libraries were also listed and located. With the completion of *Pre-1956 Imprints*, the "LC Catalog" has been converted into a union catalog. Now you can trace any work through the two catalogs described below: *Pre-1956 Imprints* and the ongoing *NUC* [1956-]. The supplement to *Pre-1956 Imprints*, volumes 686-754, should also be consulted, for these contain information gathered since the beginning of the *NUC* project in 1967. The *NUC* is available in microform and on-line.[3]

Contents (*Pre-1956 Imprints*):

1. Selected entries from the collections of major research libraries in the U.S. and Canada (the most important, of course, being the Library of Congress, which holds the copyright privilege).
2. Reprints of works whose originals have been cataloged are sometimes omitted.
3. Rare items in other collections.[4]
4. Only works printed or manuscripts written before 1956.
5. Works in all languages.
6. Books, pamphlets, maps, atlases, and music; some periodicals and other serials.[5]
7. Extensive bibliographical data: authors and their dates, full title, edition,[6] place and date of publication, pagination, special features (e.g., maps, bibliography), historical notes where relevant, LC subject classification, LC number, and copyright number. The contents of composite works and periodicals are often analyzed at length.
8. Locations: based upon some seven hundred North American libraries; if no locations are designated, it may be assumed that the work is available at the Library of Congress.

Arrangement:

1. Detailed instructions for use, Vol. 1, pp. xi-xix.

2. Alphabetical by author;[7] under the author listing, usually alphabetical by title. Some title entries where no author is indicated.
3. Anonymous works entered under the supplied authors with cross-references to title entries.[8]
4. Extensive added entries for co-authors, editors, translators, etc. as well as cross-references.
5. Locating symbols on endpapers of each volume.

Below are described notable dissimilarities between *Pre-1956 Imprints* and the *NUC* [1956-]:

Contents and Arrangement (*NUC*, 1956-):

1. Works for which cards have been printed from 1956 on, regardless of the dates of the publications themselves.
2. *Register of Additional Locations*: constituted by the last volumes of each *NUC* quinquennial cumulation.
3. Explanation of entry form and locating symbols only at the front of the first volume of each cumulation.

Review Questions:

1. What is a national union catalog? How is it useful to students of literature?
2. When was the "LC Catalog" first converted into a national catalog?
3. To what do the dates used in the LC's or *NUC*'s titles refer?
4. Is every book in every major library in the United States and Canada entered in *Pre-1956 Imprints* and its *NUC* continuation?
5. What publications other than books are entered?
6. Are only English-language works entered?
7. If no location symbols appear for an entry, is the work widely available?
8. Are main entries arranged by author, title, or subject?
9. Is a subject listing of the LC entries available?
10. Describe the extent of the bibliographical data you would expect to find for *Pre-1956 Imprints* or *NUC* main entries published in the twentieth century.
11. For which of the following would you expect to find entries in *Pre-1956 Imprints*:

a. a nineteenth-century edition of Defoe's *Robinson Crusoe* acquired by the Library of Congress shortly after its publication?
b. a first edition of Hemingway's *For Whom the Bell Tolls* (1940)?
c. a first edition of a sixteenth-century English Bible acquired by the Huntington Library prior to 1956, but not held by the Library of Congress?
d. a first edition of Nathanael West's *Miss Lonelyhearts* (1933)?

12. For which of the following would you expect to find entries in the *NUC* [1956-]:
    a. John Fowles's *The French Lieutenant's Woman* (1969)?
    b. a 1963 reprint of an English translation of Dostoyevsky's *Notes from Underground*?
    c. an important post-1956 anthology of poetry in Japanese?
    d. a University of Minnesota pamphlet by Robert E. Spiller on James Fenimore Cooper (1965)?
13. Is the British Library *General Catalogue* a national union catalog?

Research Problems:

1. Cite the full title, author, and imprint of Charles Kingsley's *The Tutor's Story*. Which American library holds the original British edition?
2. In 1924 what important avant-garde press reprinted T. S. Eliot's essay on Andrew Marvell? Which American libraries hold copies of this reprinting? Where was the essay originally published? Cite issue and page reference.
3. Using the *NUC*, prepare a list of foreign translations published in the 1960s of Gregory Corso's writings. What specific works does each volume of translation contain? Locate copies of these translations in American libraries.
4. Who was the first English translator of Emile Zola's *La Terre*? Under what title is the novel known in English?
5. Which of V. S. Pritchett's works were reprinted between 1973 and 1977? Which new books of his were published? Which include bibliographies? Who are Pritchett's chief English, American, and Canadian publishers?

6. Give full publishing information for *Slavic Studies*, published in 1972 as part of the Essay Index Reprint Series. Whom does the anthology honor? Who wrote the essay on Czech literature?

Notes (*NUC*)

1. Great Britain's national library is now the British Library, formerly called the British Museum. The British Museum *General Catalogue of Printed Books* (S44) is, however, just that and not a union catalog.
2. Dates used in the *Library of Congress*'s or *National Union Catalog*'s titles refer to the year in which library cards were printed for the books entered, not to when those books were published (although, especially after 1942, the year of card printing and the year of publication may often coincide). Thus, if in 1958 the Library of Congress—or some other major North American library—received a book printed in 1768, that book will appear in the 1958 *NUC* cumulation.

   Although the "LC Catalog" is now superseded, a brief discussion of its history may be useful. Prior to the printing of this catalog in 1942, the only record of Library Congress holdings consisted of a card file at the Library of Congress itself, copies of which were deposited in a number of major research libraries throughout the United States. The "LC Catalog" was compiled to make this record more accessible—a record more comprehensive than that of any other single American library, since the Library of Congress is legally entitled to receive all books copyrighted in the United States and since its holdings of foreign works are also most extensive. The catalog is a reprinting of cards for books received by July 31, 1942. (It includes, in addition, some books held by the Library of Congress for which cards had not been printed as well as some cards for books in other American libraries but not in the Library of Congress.) The amount of information on the card may differ, depending on the time of printing. For information on more recent cards, see *Contents* #7 above.
3. If your library lacks ongoing *NUC* volumes, fiche, or on-line capacity, the *Cumulative Book Index* (S45) may be helpful.

4. For further coverage, see *Subject Collections: A Guide to Special Book Collections and Subject Emphases as Reported by University, College, Public, and Special Libraries and Museums in the United States and Canada*, comp. Lee Ash and William G. Miller, 7th ed. rev. and enl., 2 vols. (New Providence, NJ: Bowker, 1993; and the quarterly journal *Special Collections* (1980-).
5. More comprehensive serial coverage can be found in *Ulrich's International Periodicals Directory* (S65); also see the Introduction to vol. 1 of *Pre-1956 Imprints*, p. xi. The Library of Congress prepares ongoing union catalogs of many excluded categories, e.g., music, phonorecords, motion pictures, film strips, video recordings, etc. Also available are a *NUC of Manuscript Collections* and a *National Register of Microform Masters* (1965-83); thereafter see *NUC: Books* and *New Serial Titles* (1953-).
6. Included are separate entries for different editions and issues.
7. For a subject listing, see *The Library of Congress Catalogs: Subject Catalog* (S46); for a title listing, see *Cumulative Title Index to the Library of Congress Shelflist* (Arlington, VA: Carrollton, 1983).
8. Note that the *NUC* is an important source of attributions.

M23. Jackson, W. A., F. S. Ferguson, and Katherine F. Pantzer, eds. *A Short-Title Catalogue of Books Printed in England, Scotland, and Ireland and of English Books Printed Abroad 1475-1640. First Compiled by A. W. Pollard and G. R. Redgrave.* 2nd ed., rev. and enl. London: Bibliographical Society, 1976-91. 3 vols.

This *Short* [abridged] *Title Catalogue* facilitates literary scholarship by listing and locating many extant early English publications.[1] The formal revision of the first (1926) *STC* began in 1948. The new *STC* is a vital part of the British national bibliography, i.e., a collection of bibliographies offering a near-complete record of the publications printed in a country—and often concerning that country—from the beginning of printing to the present time.

Contents (Vols. 1 and 2):

1. Extant books, including all forms of printed matter (bookplates, broadsides, etc.), published between 1475 and 1640 in the British Isles.[2]
2. All books in English, Irish, or Welsh wherever printed.[3]
3. Abridged or "short" titles of books entered.
4. Extensive bibliographical information: generally includes names of authors, translators, editors, subjects of bibliographies, persons attacked, as well as a description of the book's format (folio, octavo, etc.), the printer's name, place of publication,[4] and year of entry in the *Stationers' Register*, and a listing of the works authorized printers (stationers) intended to print.
5. Notes various editions, impressions, issues, etc.
6. Locates up to ten copies, half in the British Isles, the others mainly in the United States but also in Australia and New Zealand; the *STC* listings are not a complete census, however.[5]

Arrangement (Vols. 1 and 2):

1. Introduction: a detailed user's guide, 1: xix-xliii.
2. Abbreviations and symbols: libraries, reference works, and owners, 1: xliv-liii.
3. Alphabetical arrangement by author's name or initials (if no name).[6]
4. Anonymous works: listed under author's name if author has been identified; otherwise, listed under the first proper name in the title or, if there is no proper name, under the first substantive.
5. Unofficial writings bearing the name of a monarch are entered under his or her name; acts (or explanations of acts, i.e., regulations) pertaining to London are entered under London, to England under England, etc.
6. Entry numbers for all main entries; entry numbers for some variant editions and issues.
7. *STC* entry numbers at top of page; page numbers at bottom.
8. Cross-references: by entry number.
9. Addenda at back of each volume.

Contents and Arrangement (Volume 3):

1. Its own table of contents, introductory material, and abbreviations.
2. Index of printers' and publishers' names that appear in the imprints—chronologically arranged with cross-references to *STC* citations.
3. Appendices following this first section: special titles (e.g., those whose sale proceeds benefit needy stationers, names of members of the stationers' company).
4. Brief biographies provided or located.
5. Index by place of publication (British Isles and Colonies, the Continent, fictitious places).
6. Other London indexes and index of anomalous imprints.
7. Further Addenda and Corrigenda for vols. 1 and 2.
8. Fold-out map of London in the sixteenth century to enable the locating of printers.
9. Index by year of publication.

Review Questions:

1. What is the *Stationer's Register*?
2. For which of the following would you expect to find entries: Holinshed's *Chronicles* (a source for many of Shakespeare's plays); a regulation concerning tithing by the Anglican Church; Giovanni Paoli Lomazzo's work on painting, published in English translation at the end of the sixteenth century; the English Jesuit John Rastell's tracts against the Church of England, published in Antwerp in the mid-sixteenth century?
3. What sort of bibliographical information does the *STC* provide?
4. If no place of publication is entered, where was the work published?
5. What is the *STC*'s main principle of arrangement?
6. How can the *STC* be helpful to researchers who lack access to libraries that hold original editions?
7. What separately published indexes to the *STC* are available?

Research Problems:

1. How many separate editions of *Love's Labor's Lost* appeared during Shakespeare's lifetime (1564-1616)? Under what cover title did this edition appear? Who printed it? Where can the original volume be seen?
2. When and by whom were these anonymous ballads first printed: "This maide would give tenne shillings for a kisse" and "Fond love why dost thou dally: or the passionate lovers ditty"? When was the following anonymous work entered in the *Stationers' Register*, and where can an original copy be seen: "The forme and shape of a monstrous child borne at Maydstone"? (See "Maidstone.")
3. What work of Jacques Cartier's was published in England in the sixteenth century? Cite the English translator, printer, and year and place of publication; describe the format of the book. What British libraries hold original copies?
4. List English-language works by or about Roger Bacon published before 1640. To make your list more complete, what kind of index would be most helpful? When was Robert Greene's historical comedy about Friar Bacon and Friar Bungay first published? Who published the second edition?
5. What do we know about the life William Barley [Barlow], a London bookseller (i.e., publisher), led prior to 1600? What is the title of the quarto concerning Judith Philips that he sold in 1595?
6. Where can one find the first printing of Edward VI's deathbed prayer? (Edward died on 6 July 1553.) Cite the anonymous ballad rejoicing over the supposed pregnancy of his sister Mary I, Queen of England.

Notes (*STC*)

1. Pollard's original warning that the *STC* is "a dangerous work for anyone to handle lazily, that is, without verification" (vii) still stands, however.

   Reference works based on the *STC* include A. F. Allison and V. F. Goldsmith, *Titles of English Books (And of Foreign Books Printed in England): An Alphabetical Finding List by Title of Books Published under the Author's Name, Pseudonym or Initials,*

Vol. 1 (1475-1640 (Hamden, CT: Shoe String; Folkestone, Kent: Dawson, 1976); William Warner Bishop, *A Checklist of American Copies of "Short-Title Catalogue" Books*, 2nd ed. (Ann Arbor: U of Michigan P, 1950; rpt. NY: Greenwood, 1968); and David Ramage, *A Finding-List of English Books to 1640 in Libraries in the British Isles* (Durham, Eng.: Council of the Durham Colleges, 1958).

2. The British national bibliography can be constructed from the following works:

Arber, Edward. *A Transcript of Registers of the Company of Stationers of London, 1554-1640 A.D.* 5 vols. 1875-94; rpt. New York: Peter Smith, 1950. (Largely superseded by the *STC*; it does, however, include nonextant books.)

Wing, Donald. *Short-Title Catalogue of Books Printed in England, Scotland, Ireland, Wales, and British America and of English Books Printed in Other Countries 1641-1700.* (S49.)

[Eyre, G. E. B.] *A Transcript of the Registers of the Worshipful Company of Stationers from 1640-1708 A.D.* 3 vols. 1913-14; rpt. New York: Peter Smith, 1950.

Arber, Edward. *The Term Catalogues, 1668-1709 A.D., with a Number for the Easter Term 1711 A. D.: A Contemporary Bibliography of English Literature in the Reigns of Charles II, James II, William and Mary, and Anne.* 3 vols. 1903-06; rpt. New York: Johnson Reprint, 1965. (A contemporary list edited from London booksellers' quarterly lists.)

The Eighteenth-Century Short-Title Catalogue 1990 (ESTC 1990). London: British Library, 1990 [microfiche]. This is a part of the in-progress *ESTC* database, ed. Robin Alston (London: British Library; Baton Rouge: Louisiana State U, 1984-).

The English Catalogue of Books. . . . London: [various publishers for original and reprint editions, 1801-1969]. (Based on lists appearing in a trade journal, *The Publisher*, successor to the *Publishers' Circular* and *British Books*.)

Whitaker's Books in Print: The Reference Catalogue of Current Literature. London: Whitaker, 1874-.

Whitaker's Book List: A Classified List of Publications. London: Whitaker, 1924-. (Cumulation of lists published in the trade journals *The Bookseller* and *Current Literature*.)

The British National Bibliography. London: Council of the British National Bibliography, 1950-. (Considered the best current national bibliography.)

Cumulative Book Index: A World List of Books in the English Language. (S45.)

3. Also included are all Latin service-books, wherever printed, between 1475 and 1640, for use in England and Scotland. See the introduction to volume 1, pp. xxii-xxviii for unusual inclusions.
4. If no place of publication is given, the work was published in London. A query after the note of entry refers not to the date but to the identity of the book.
5. Most works listed are available on microfilm; see *Early English Books 1475-1640* (Ann Arbor, MI: University Microfilms, [1938—]). See Bishop's *Checklist* and Ramage's *Finding-List* (note 1, above), for further locations.
6. See note 1 for Allison and Goldsmith's title index.

M24. Evans, Charles. *American Bibliography: A Chronological Dictionary of All Books, Pamphlets, and Periodical Publications Printed in the United States of America from the Genesis of Printing in 1639 Down to and Including the Year 1800 with Bibliographical and Biographical Notes.* 12 vols. 1903-34; rpt. New York: Peter Smith, 1941; rpt. in one volume—Metuchen, NJ: Mini-Print, 1967. [Actually reaches only to 1799; completed through 1800 by Clifford Shipton under the title *The American Bibliography of Charles Evans . . .* (1955; rpt. Worcester, MA: American Antiquarian Society, 1962) and indexed by Roger Pattrell Bristol under Shipton's title (Worcester, MA: American Antiquarian Society, 1959). Shipton and Bristol's additions constitute vols. 13 and 14 of "Evans."]

Bristol, Roger P. *Supplement to Charles Evans' American Bibliography.* Charlottesville, VA: University Press of Virginia, 1970. [*Index to Supplement* (1971) both an author-title index and an index of printers, publishers, and booksellers.][1]

Like the *STC* (M23), Evans is a retrospective listing of the first works in a national bibliography. As such it is a valuable source for studies in early American literature. Because of its chronological arrangement, this work may be regarded as a literary history in bibliographic form. The first few pages of Evans's preface make fascinating—often inspirational—reading. Here Evans not only presents a capsule history of the United States implicit in American printed documents but also movingly expresses the love of books and country that underlie his thirty-five-year labor compiling the *American Bibliography.*

Contents:

1. Virtually all printed matter published in America between 1639 and 1800:[2] includes periodicals and newspapers under every year in which they were published.
2. Bibliographical information: full title and subtitle,[3] author's full name with birth and death dates, and bibliographic description including imprint [printer and/or publisher, and place and date of publication found at the bottom of the title page], paging, and format.[4]
3. Bibliographical and biographical annotation.
4. Some cursory locating of entries.[5]
5. Historical and literary surveys preceding vols. 1-5.
6. Author, subject, and printer indexes.

Arrangement:

1. Chronological; alphabetical by author's name within the year of publication, with anonymous works found under the attributed author's name.
2. Numbered entries.[6]
3. Separate author, anonymous title, and subject indexes at the back of each volume; for authors and titles, use volume 14's index instead.
4. Directory of printers and publishers at the back of vols. 1-12, arranged by town in vol. 1, thereafter by state; but see note 1.

5. Comprehensive author-title index, vol. 14. Since names of people, ships, and Indian tribes appearing in titles are entered, to some extent vol. 14 can also serve as a subject index.[7]

Review Questions:

1. Why does Evans call his work a "Dictionary"?
2. Through what year does its coverage extend?
3. In what respects is the *American Bibliography* similar to the *STC*? In what respects is it different?
4. Where are the indexes to Evans?

Research Problems:

1. What was the first work printed in America? Where was it printed, by whom, and in what form?
2. What were the first two Shakespearean plays printed in America? Where and when were they printed? When was *Hamlet* first printed in America? In what form was it printed? Was *Paradise Lost* printed in America before or after *Hamlet*?
3. How many separate prints of Michael Wigglesworth's *Day of Doom* were published before 1700? Give full publishing information for the 1670 printing.
4. List, in chronological order, works published in America before 1800 on Henry II's lover, Fair Rosamond.
5. What work having to do with marriage was printed by Samuel Hall of Newport, Rhode Island, in 1765?
6. What works by Jean-Jacques Rousseau were printed in America before 1800?

Notes (Evans)

1. In addition, Bristol has prepared an *Index to Printers, Publishers, and Booksellers Indicated by Charles Evans in His American Bibliography* (Charlottesville, VA: U of Virginia P, 1961), which takes precedence over the directory of printers and publishers in vols. 1-12. Also see Clifford K. Shipton and James E. Mooney, *National Index of American Imprints Through 1800: The Short-*

Title Evans, 2 vols. ([Worcester, MA]: American Antiquarian Society and Barre, 1969).

2. Our American national bibliography can be constructed from the following works:

Sabin, Joseph. *Bibliotheca Americana; A Dictionary of Books Relating to America, from its Discovery to the Present Time* [to 1892] (S48).

Shaw, Ralph R., and Richard H. Shoemaker. *American Bibliography: A Preliminary Checklist* [1801-19]. 2 vols. New York: Scarecrow, 1958-66.

Roorbach, O. A. *Bibliotheca Americana: Catalogue of American Publications 1820*-[1861]. 4 vols., 1852-61; rpt. New York: Peter Smith, 1939; rpt. in one volume (with Kelly—see below—Metuchen, NJ: Mini-Print, 1967). (Many inaccuracies; superseded for the years covered to date by Shoemaker's *Checklist* below.)

Shoemaker, Richard H. [et al.]. *A Checklist of American Imprints*. Ed. Carol Rinderknecht and Scott Bruntjen. New York [later Metuchen, NJ]: Scarecrow, 1964-. (Currently covers from 1820 through 1845; when complete, Shoemaker's work will replace Roorbach.)

Kelly, James. *The American Catalogue of Books* [1861-71]. 2 vols. 1866-71; rpt. New York: Peter Smith, 1938; rpt. in one volume (with Roorbach—see above)—Metuchen, NJ: Mini-Print, 1967. (Many inaccuracies.)

American Book Publishing Record (ABPR). New York: Bowker, 1960-. Microfiche. (Both ongoing and retrospective to 1876 with corrections; some exclusions.) Uncorrected paper sources for *ABPR* include the following:

Publishers Weekly. New York: Bowker, 1872-.

The American Catalogue of Books [1876-1910]. 13 vols. 1880-1911; rpt. New York: Peter Smith, 1941. (Based on lists of new books appearing in *Publishers Weekly*.)

The Publishers' Trade List Annual. New York: Bowker, 1873-. (Indexed since 1948 in *Books in Print* [M29].)

Cumulative Book Index [1898-] (S45).

United States Catalogue. Minneapolis [later New York: Wilson, 1899. (Replaced the *American Catalogue of Books* [1876-1910].)

3. But Shipton uses short titles in his volume 13 because of high printing costs.
4. *American Bibliography*, like its British counterparts, must be used warily. The accuracy of some 30 percent of Evans's entries has been questioned.
5. Evans's location initials are identified by John C. Munger in *Bulletin of the New York Public Library* 40 (1936): 665-68. In his preface to volume 13 of *The American Bibliography*, Shipton points out that Evans's minimal locating does not necessarily attest to the rarity of the books cited.
6. This "Evans number" is important for finding the full texts in Readex's microcard *Early American Imprints, Series I: Evans*, which also includes titles more recently discovered.
7. Newspapers and almanacs are listed not under their titles but under the headings "newspapers" and "almanacs," under "N" and "A."

GENERAL REVIEW 2

1. What is the literary importance of the *Epistola Cuthberti de Obitu Bedae*? What historical transformation is revealed by the poem it contains? Who has written the standard study of Cuthbert's letter? Where can you find a modern edition of the "Death Song"?

2. Using a specialized serial bibliography, note the kinds of theory Ros Ballaster uses and to what end she uses them in her *Seductive Forms: Women's Amatory Fiction from 1684 to 1740* (1992).

3. How many important biographical, political, and critical treatments of Sir Walter Raleigh appeared in the seventeenth century? Where can you find a modern scholarly discussion of Raleigh's marriage?

4. What French, Italian, and Greek works influenced the *Erotokritos*? When was the *Erotokritos* first published? When was its importance first recognized? Who translated it in the later 1920s?

5. Cite a "Who's Who" reference work, the first edition of which appeared in the 1970s, devoted to biographies of outstanding contemporary black Americans. About how many entries did the first edition contain?

6. What was Faulkner's last novel? What is it about? What significant political and scientific events took place in the year of its publication?

7. Which British collectors hold original copies of the English translation of Ludwig Lavatar's "Of ghostes and spirites walking

by nyght" (printed 1572)? What other works by Lavatar were translated into English and published in the sixteenth century?

8. List the works of the scholar Merritt Hughes, published between 1965 and 1968. (Supply full bibliographical information, and explain all abbreviations.)

9. Under what title was the London edition of Harold Frederic's *The Damnation of Theron Ware* (an American novel) first issued? What was the British publisher's source for this title?

10. Who is the only antebellum Southerner currently regarded as a major national writer? Mention two ways in which he rejects regionalism in his fiction. What system of social organization did Southerners mythologize and glorify?

11. Prepare a primary bibliography of the plays of Maxwell Anderson (an American) published in the 1940s. Prepare a bibliography of critical articles about *Winterset*. (Explain all abbreviations.)

12. What two jokes did Sir Thomas More make just before his execution? In what work was More first associated with two other Catholic saints? (Cite place and year of publication.)

13. List all the bibliographies of George Eliot, regardless of the form in which they appeared, published between 1963 and 1967.

14. When was the Anglo-Irish writer, William Trevor, made a CBE? What *is* a CBE? What did Trevor write in 1994? How can he be reached?

15. Which of Carson McCullers's works have been filmed? Which have been adapted for the stage? When (month, day, year) did Carson McCullers die? Which periodicals contain her obituary?

16. Where did Henry V achieve a resounding victory against the French? In which of Shakespeare's plays does Falstaff appear?

17. In what year was the first almanac printed in New England? The "Bay Psalm Book"? The first publication of Harvard College? The first spelling book?

18. What is "cubist poetry"? Name four writers whose works could be described as cubist.

19. Cite a bibliography published in 1937 of famous literary works set in England's Lake District. Of what series is this bibliography a part? How many literary works are entered? Account for the paucity of entries.

20. Name two critics who, between 1989 and 1990, have written explicatory studies of Malamud's "The Prison." In what work can Lois Lamdin's earlier piece on "Malamud's Schlemiels" be found?

21. How is New Historicism theoretically opposed to orthodox scholarship? Who were the first editors of the journal *Representations*? Which of these editors was a specialist in American literature? Who wrote the entry you are drawing upon, and where does he teach?

22. In 1964 John Barth wrote a piece for the New American Library edition of a famous eighteenth-century novel. Name the novel. What was Barth's contribution to this edition? What other works by Barth were first published in 1964?

23. Distinguish between two kinds of dirges in Greek literature. Name two Greek writers of dirges. What literary work provides the earliest evidence for such dirges?

24. When was "trigger" first used as a verb in the sense of "to cause" or "to activate"? Give the full name of the writer whose work is cited. Who coined the phrase "nouveau poor"? Where and when did it appear?

25. What is a zoom shot? A point of view shot? Formative theory?

26. What are the seven deadly sins? The original seven wonders of the world? Who are the seven sleepers of Ephesus?

27. Give the complete title and publishing information for the earliest American book about Dr. Faustus.

28. Whose work has been particularly influential in joining theory and pedagogy in the United States? In which of his works does he suggest making critical conflict itself a course subject? (State the full title of the essay.) In whose anthology do contributors consider how the "'scene of instruction' poses theoretically significant questions about power and expertise"?

29. Who are some of the women poets published in the Yale Series of Younger Poets? Where was the original Tin Pan Alley, and what composers were associated with it?

30. In what languages are there etymologically related forms of the word "mother"?

31. Where was John Harvard, the principal founder of Harvard College, born? Where was his mother born? What business property did she leave to John? What was his first professional position in New England? What did he bequeath to the proposed college that was to bear his name?

32. Using a specialized serial bibliography, note what Berndt Astendorf regards as essential for understanding black American literature (*Black Literature in White America*, 1982).

33. Give complete publishing information for an American edition of *Les Miserables* edited by someone known to us only by his initials: H. L. A.

34. Who was Joan Plowright's second husband? What films did Plowright make in 1991 and 1992? What does her brother do?

35. According to Edmund Wilson, how is Lincoln's plea for the rule of law prophetic? In 1932 who were co-signers with Wilson of an open letter backing the Communist presidential ticket?

36. What is the title of Elaine Showalter's critical survey article in *The Ontario Review* (1984)?

37. What are Conrad's three greatest short pieces? Which was "a feat of memory"? In what respect is Conrad like Henry James? Whose critical opinions are you following?

38. The following work was published in 1525: *Here foloweth a lytell treatyse of the Beaute of women.* From what language was it translated? In what format was it originally published? Where can the first edition be seen in the United States?

39. Cite an article published in 1979 containing a four-page unannotated bibliography on structuralism as a mode of literary analysis.

40. What works written between 1916 and 1970 deal with the reception of American literature in Russia, i.e., with "American books abroad"?

41. How much of Griswold's *Illustrated Life of Washington* was written by Griswold? When did Lossing's name first appear on the title page? In how many parts was the *Life* originally issued? How frequently did the parts appear? Over what years did they appear?

42. Where can you find a list of the books that Somerset Maugham donated to King's School in Canterbury? Cite two separately published Maugham bibliographies—one primary, one secondary—that appeared in the 1970s. When was the first edition of Toole-Stott's work published?

43. Cite a reference work on movies made between 1928 and 1991 that were adapted from books and plays. Cite a 1987 edition of a catalog of movies made for television.

44. List the works of the poet Ovid. Which is his only surviving work in hexameters? Which of his lost works was praised by Quintilian and Tactitus? Which famous English playwright translated his *Amores*?

45. When was the Basque epic *The Song of Lelo* composed? What movement aroused interest in the Basques? Who wrote Garoa, and what does it deal with? Who are "Xabier de Lizard" and "Orixe"?

46. What works have tentatively been attributed to Smollett? To what periodicals did Smollett contribute?

47. What was poet Anne Sexton's first job? What poem by another writer made the deepest impression upon her? Which is her best-known book? Which of her works were published in the two years following her death?

48. Cite an explicatory article on Jackson's "The Lottery" that appeared in *American Literature*. Where can you find Lenemaja Friedman's explication of "The Lottery"?

CHAPTER 4

ABSTRACTS, INDEXES, AND DIRECTORIES

M25. *Dissertation Abstracts International* and *Comprehensive Dissertation Index*

M26. *Film Literature Index*

M27. *Essay and General Literature Index*

M28. *Book Review Index*

M29. *Books in Print*, *Subject Guide to Books in Print*, and *Books in Print Supplement*

M30. *MLA Directory of Periodicals*

A compilation of abstracts may be regarded as an index that lists, locates, and, most important, briefly describes longer studies. Indexes, whether designed to analyze the contents of particular publications or to search miscellaneous publications for particular literary genres or subjects, are among the most important locating tools. A directory is essentially an alphabetically arranged listing of persons, places, organizations, or publications. The *MLA Directory of Periodicals* is especially useful if you are trying to find journals likely to be interested in publishing your own scholarly or creative writings. When you consider the enormous proliferation of literary publication in recent years, the value of abstracts, indexes, and directories at once becomes evident.

M25. *Dissertation Abstracts International: Abstracts of Dissertations Available on Microfilm or as Xerographic Reproductions*. [Ann Arbor]: University Microfilms International, 1938-. [Formerly *Microfilm Abstracts* (1938-51); *Dissertation Abstracts* (1952-69).]

Comprehensive Dissertation Index 1861-1972. 37 vols. Ann Arbor: University Microfilms International, 1973. [Annual supplements.]

DAI is a monthly compilation of abstracts (i.e., summaries, often chapter by chapter, of about 350 words written by the dissertation authors) of American, Canadian, some British, and a few foreign doctoral dissertations. Abstracts are time-savers; on the one hand, since you can quickly determine which studies are relevant to your own special interests, you need consult only those; on the other hand, abstracts can help you keep abreast of far more criticism than you could hope to read in its entirety.[1] You may order dissertations through interlibrary loan (it's wise to express a preference for paper over microform), or purchase any dissertation for which an order number is noted from University Microfilms International.[2] Examining the thorough and up-to-date bibliographies of recent dissertations can be especially valuable for your research.

The *CDI*, a keyword-in-title and author index, makes the finding of abstracts almost effortless. An average of six principal words in the dissertation title are indexed alphabetically. For example, if you wish to locate a recent dissertation on Australian novelists, checking under either substantive in the 1993 Supplement will turn up Elisabeth J. Köster's "'Operating from Bastard Territory': Attitudes toward the Motherland and the Colonial Self in Four Australian and Canadian Novelists" (The University of Western Ontario [Canada], 1991, 299 pages) with references to the volume, issue, and page number of *Dissertation Abstracts* in which the abstract appears. The order number is also provided. (The same information can be found under "Köster" in *CDI*'s author index volumes.) Because coverage extends, in some cases, from the very first Ph.D. dissertations written in the United States to the present time, and also includes locating entries for most non-abstracted dissertations, *CDI* largely eliminates the need to search indexes in more specialized works.[3] Also, perusing *CDI* can tell you quite a bit about critical trends, past and present.

The following descriptions and review questions are based on *DAI*'s 1993 format and on the format of the first edition of *CDI* with its *1993 Supplement*. (*DAI* is now available on-line.)

Contents (*DAI*):

1. Abstracts of dissertations written at most American and Canadian institutions, a considerable number of British universities from 1988 on, and a negligible number of foreign universities—some 550 in all, as of 1993.[4]
2. Relevant information: author, title, university, year of acceptance, supervisor (in some cases), length, and order number.
3. Indexes: both Keyword Title Index and Author [of dissertation] Index for each monthly issue, cumulated annually through vol. 33 (1972-73); thereafter, only author indexes are cumulated annually as Part II of Issue 12.[5]

Arrangement (each issue of *DAI*):

1. Division into three parts:
   Part A—Humanities and Social Sciences.
   Part B—The Sciences and Engineering (division begins with vol. 27, no. 1 (July 1966).
   Part C—Worldwide (formerly *European Abstracts*).[6]
   Each section is paginated separately. Identical page numbers are distinguished by the section letters (A, B, or C) that precede them.
2. Table of contents (an alphabetically ordered subject classification).
3. Introduction and ordering information for copies of Master's theses and doctoral dissertations.[7]
4. List of subject categories.
5. List of participating institutions.

6. Abstract entries: within the category or subcategory (see Table of Contents) entries arranged alphabetically by author of dissertation.
7. Keyword title index followed by author index.

Contents and Arrangement (*CDI*—Literature and Language vols. and author index):

1. Literature and Language: vols. 29 (A-L) and 30 (M-Z).
2. Clarification of keyword entry style and sample entries, pp. xi-xiv.[8]
3. Schools Included, p. xv-xvii.
4. Keyword index: arranged alphabetically by keyword; note cross-references to related broad subject headings—e.g., Biography and Theatre, both in vol. 31—at the beginning of the Language and Literature volume.
5. Relevant information: under the keyword entry—title, author, degree, year awarded, conferring institution, length of dissertation, locating reference, and order number (if available from University Microfilms International).
6. Author index, vols. 33-37. Alphabetically arranged by last name of author; entries duplicate those in (5) above.

Contents and Arrangement (*CDI 1993 Suppl.*):

1. Annual supplement in five volumes.
2. Language and Literature Keyword index in vol. 4 (Social Sciences and Humanities, Part 2).
3. Cumulative Author [of Dissertation] Index for 1993 in vol. 5.

Review Questions:

1. How "international" is *DAI*'s coverage?
2. How far back do abstracts for American dissertations go?
3. In what ways are abstracts valuable?
4. Currently, how much does a paperbound xerographic copy of an American or Canadian dissertation cost?
5. What subject matter is covered in Part A of *DAI*? How are dissertation abstracts arranged within Part A?
6. Does *CDI* index only those dissertations abstracted in *DAI*?

How does a keyword-in-title index work?

7. Which volumes of *CDI* cover Literature and Language? Which volumes of *CDI* contain the cumulative author index? How often do *CDI* supplements appear?

Research Problems:

1. Cite a dissertation accepted in 1983 comparing Sam Shepard with three other contemporary playwrights. How did Christopher Lasch characterize the era that Shepard's work reflects?
2. Name a dissertation written prior to 1971 dealing with the sources of J. R. R. Tolkien's *The Lord of the Rings* and a dissertation dealing with its structure. Cite the authors' names, the schools conferring their degrees, and the length of the dissertations.
3. On what sùbject did these eminent scholar-critics write their doctoral dissertations: Fredson T. Bowers? Maynard Mack? Robert Ornstein? If no order number for the dissertation abstract is given, note the source of your editor's citation.
4. Whose dissertations were accepted from 1975 through 1977 on Randall Jarrell? State their titles. Which of the genres that Jarrell worked in does the Yale writer study?
5. Cite a dissertation (not necessarily literary in emphasis) completed at Harvard in 1977 on Elizabethan interest in the supernatural. Has it been abstracted in *DAI*?
6. Find a dissertation entitled "Literature and the Obscenity Question." What conclusions does the writer reach about the views of judges?

Notes (*DAI-CDI*)

1. The same is true of periodical literature; see *Abstracts of English Studies* (S10); on-line substitutes for that important but currently defunct abstracting service are *Periodical Abstracts*, listing major American academic periodicals as well as general interest and business journals, and the related *Expanded Academic Index*, also limited to major American periodicals. In addition, see *Abstracts of Folklore Studies* (1963-75), *American Literature Abstracts: A Review of Current Scholarship in the Field of American Literature*

(1967-72); *College Composition and Communication*'s abstracts in its annual bibliography (S153); *Linguistics and Language Behavior Abstracts* (S154); *MLA Abstracts of Articles in Scholarly Journals* (1970-75); *Seventeenth-Century Newsletter* (1942-), which contains abstracts of recent articles on seventeenth-century English and American literary works; and *Women's Studies Abstracts* (1972-).

2. At this writing, the cost of American and Canadian dissertations to students, faculty, and other academics is $32.50 for microform, $36 for paperbound photocopies, and $43 for hard cover. British dissertations cost $74 for microform, $127.50 for paperbound photocopies, and $137.50 for hard cover.
3. Yet, because of their foreign coverage, you may still profitably consult the following works:

   Retrospective Index to Theses of Great Britain and Ireland, 1716-1950. Vol. 1: *Social Science and Humanities*. Santa Barbara, CA: ABC-Clio, 1975. Addenda, 1977.

   Index to Theses with Abstracts Accepted for Higher Degrees by the Universities of Great Britain and Ireland and the Council for National Academic Awards [1950-]. London: ASLIB, 1953-.

   Reynolds, Michael M. *A Guide to Theses and Dissertations: An International Bibliography of Bibliographies*. Rev. and enl. Phoenix, AZ: Oryx, 1985.

4. Although the number of contributing institutions, beginning with an initial five in 1938, has only gradually increased, later participants often allowed microfilming of older dissertations. Hence *CDI* may cite an order number for a dissertation not abstracted in *DAI*.
5. These annual cumulations constitute the supplements to *CDI*.
6. This category was first included in 1989. European abstracts available through University Microfilms International are also listed in sections A and B.
7. For abstracts of Master's theses, see *Masters Abstracts International* (Ann Arbor: University Microfilms, 1962-). *Index to Theses with Abstracts Accepted for Higher Degrees by the Universities of Great Britain and Ireland. . .* (see above, note 3)

is an annual title list of British Bachelor's and Master's theses, abstracted from 1986 on, as well as doctoral dissertations, all with locating annotations.

For stylistic conventions observed in most Master's theses and doctoral dissertations, see *The MLA Handbook*, currently in its fourth edition (S19).

8. Under Explanation of Entries—Citations (p. xiv) the editors note, "The prefix L. W. or X. indicates that the citation to the dissertation was obtained from *American Doctoral Dissertations* and its predecessors. . . See the list of Sources Consulted [pp.xviii-xx] for complete information."

M26. *Film Literature Index: A Quarterly Author-Subject Index to the International Periodical Literature of Film and Television/ Video*. Albany: Film and Television Documentation Center, State University of New York at Albany, 1973-.

Film Literature Index is the most extensive, ongoing, up-to-date bibliography of film criticism and reviews in selected newspapers, magazines, and scholarly journals.[1] Its only drawbacks are its recent inception and the unavoidable constraints on the number of periodicals analyzed.[2]

Contents:

1. Articles are analyzed in more than 300 international periodicals, both specialized and general interest.
2. Articles in "exotic or fugitive" periodicals (Preface.)
3. Includes film reviews, festivals, film and TV history and theory, study and teaching of film,[3] bibliographies, filmographies, interviews, obituaries, technical and financial aspects.
4. Excludes fan magazines, solely technical writings, and brief press releases.
5. Information provided: original title (followed by an **f**), American title if different, director (preceded by **d**), date of first showing, national provenance.
6. Quarterly issues cumulated annually.[4]

Arrangement:

1. Abbreviations and Periodicals Indexed at front.
2. Two sections: Film and Television/Video.
3. Each alphabetically arranged section combines author of article, title, and subject.
4. Name entries and cross-references for authors of articles, screenwriters, performers, directors, cinematographers, professional societies, and corporations.
5. Geographic names appear as subheadings under specific subject headings.[5]
6. Particular festivals found under the subject heading "Festivals."

Review Questions:

1. Which of the following would you expect to find indexed: reviews of a 1991 video production of Prokofiev's opera *War and Peace*; a review of a university-made film documentary on preserving Yiddish theater; a 1991 article in the *New York Times* on the role of linguistics in moviemaking; an article in a Hungarian periodical on Andy Warhol; a 1960s essay on *Gone with the Wind*?
2. Under what heading would you look for a French essay on the teaching of screenwriting in China?
3 Can you use *FLI* to find out when a film or video was made?

Research Problems:

1. Who wrote what seems to be the longest article listed in the 1992 *FLI* on Derek Jarman's *Edward II*? Where did the article appear? (Cite full periodical title and city of publication.) Cite an article dealing with Jarman's adaptation of Marlowe's play and an article on the screenplay itself. Is either illustrated?
2. Find a 1973 review of a film based on a play by Racine and directed by Pierre Jourdan. Supply full publication information.
3. Which of Dickens's novels was not listed in *FLI* until 1990, although it was adapted for Masterpiece Theatre in 1989? How would you explain the time lag?
4. Locate a *New York Times* review of *The Remains of the Day* published in January 1993. Which other films by its director were

reviewed in a Canadian periodical in September 1992? Supply full publication information.

5. By checking the 1991 "cultural" subject headings, locate a discussion of the English television broadcast of John Berger's "Ways of Seeing."
6. Locate a 1977 article in *Variety* on Metro-Goldwyn-Mayer's intention of making an Ernest Hemingway movie. Who was slated to direct?

Notes (*FLI*)

1. Essays in books about film are analyzed in Rehrauer's *Macmillan Film Bibliography* (S118) and Frank Manchel's *Film Study: An Analytical Bibliography* (S118).
2. A number of bibliographies provide coverage prior to 1973. For pieces written through 1935, see *The Film Index: A Bibliography*, 3 vols. (White Plains, NY: Kraus, 1941-85), an annotated subject guide. For the intervening period before the establishment of *FLI*, see *Index to Critical Film Reviews in British and American Periodicals, Together with: Index to Critical Reviews of Books about Film*, ed. Stephen E. Bowles, 3 vols. in 2 (New York: Franklin, 1974-75), a title index. For coverage of periodicals omitted from *FLI*, see the *International Index to Film Periodicals* (S127). An excellent guide to American reference sources, mostly from 1960 on, is *On the Screen: A Film, Television, and Video Research Guide* (S122).
3. Of special interest to students of literature are Ross Harris, *Film as Literature, Literature as Film: An Introduction to and Bibliography of Film's Relationship to Literature*. Bibliographies and Indexes in World Literature, Number 10 (New York: Greenwood, 1987; and Jeffrey Egan Welch, *Literature and Film: An Annotated Bibliography, 1909-77* (New York: Garland, 1981) with *Supplement: An Annotated Bibliography, 1978-88* (1993). For primary sources see *The American Film Institute Catalog of Motion Pictures Produced in the United States* (S117) and its concise British counterpart, Dennis Gifford's *The British Film Catalogue 1895-1985: A Reference Guide* (New York: Facts on File, 1986).

4. Note that end-of-year pieces may not be picked up by *FLI* bibliographers until the following year.
5. Thus, for "Australian cinematography" see "Cinematography," following the subheading "History of Cinematography."

M27. *Essay and General Literature Index 1900-1933: An Index to Above 40,000 Essays and Articles in 2144 Volumes of Collections of Essays and Miscellaneous Works.* New York: Wilson, 1934. Supplements: 1934-74 (Vols. 2-8): thereafter, semiannual supplements bound annually and cumulated every five years.

EGLI is a subject and author index to essays in books, including essays originally published in periodicals and those originally published as parts of books. It is especially valuable as an analyzing tool for Festschriften, similar collections of essays on a variety of subjects, and chapters on disparate subjects in books.[1] *EGLI* is also useful to students of literature in that it provides up-to-date (on-line for recent years) primary and secondary bibliographies of essays in books for a given author. Authors' essays are both listed and located as are critical essays on their work in general and their individual works.

Contents:

1. Essays in books published from 1900 to date; thus essays written prior to 1900 are indexed if they have been reprinted in a twentieth-century volume.[2]
2. Essays in all fields; humanities and social sciences stressed; film and play reviews included.
3. Unannotated.
4. English-language essays only; however, foreign-language essays translated into English are included.
5. Generally indexes books by American publishers only; a few British editions are included.

Arrangement:

1. Each volume arranged alphabetically, combining author, subject, and cross-reference entries. Some title entries, especially for films, plays, and anonymous and pseudonymous works.
2. Under author entries *EGLI* lists in this order:
   a. works by the author.
   b. works about the author's life and canon.
   c. criticisms of individual works.[3]
3. Cross-references from pseudonyms and subjects.
4. Subject entries arranged alphabetically by author within the subheading.
5. List of Books Indexed (citing full bibliographical information except for place of publication) at back of each volume; arranged alphabetically by author, editor, and title, with cross-references to the main entry.
6. From volume 7 on, the Directory of Publishers and Distributors follows the List of Books Indexed.

Review Questions:

1. For which of the following would you expect to find entries:
   a. an essay by Thomas Babington Macaulay published in 1843?
   b. an article on Tennessee Williams in the *Atlantic*?
   c. an essay on Williams in a collection entitled *The Sound of Self-Parody*, treating Albee, Miller, and Williams?
   d. the titles of all the chapters in a book by a single author, each chapter dealing with a different subject?
   e. an essay in French by Jean-Paul Sartre published in a collection of essays?
   f. a chapter treating John Updike's *Rabbit, Run*?
   g. an essay in English analyzing the work of Aleksandr Solzhenitsyn?
   h. F. R. Leavis's essay, the title of which escapes you, on *Othello*?
2. Which of the following does *EGLI* contain:
   a. annotations for the essays indexed?
   b. full bibliographical information for all books whose chapters are indexed?

c. subject headings and subdivisions?
d. cross-references from a pseudonym to the author's real name?
e. indexing of an essay published separately as a monograph?
f. a list of all the essays an author has written for a single collection?

Research Problems:

1. How many anthologies containing essays about Jacques Derrida's *Of Grammatology* were published between 1980 and 1984?
2. In the fifty years since his death, have the essays of Paul Valéry (1871-1945) on the general subject of poetry been translated into English and collected in a single volume? If so, supply the title of this volume, its translator, and the name of the critic who wrote its introduction. What is the title of the collected edition and the volume number in which these essays were published? Of what series is the collected edition a part? Cite its series volume number.
3. Locate the author of an essay on the English language entitled "English in 2061: A Forecast," published in a collection in the 1960s. Cite the title and editor of the collection, as well as the edition, the publisher, and the publication.
4. Cite two essays by John Hollander that were anthologized between 1970 and 1974. Give first names of editors, subtitles of anthologies, publishers, dates, and pages on which the essays appear.
5. Cite an essay anthologized in 1973 about a stage production of Euripdes's *Medea*. Cite two essays anthologized in the 1920s on *Medea* in performance. Where can the essays be found?
6. Locate an essay in an anthology published between 1960 and 1964 on the epic hero Beowulf and the ship discovered at Sutton Hoo. What is the full name of the essayist and the title of the essay? Cite the title of the anthology, the full name of its editor, the publisher, and date of publication. On what pages of this anthology does the essay appear?

Notes (*EGLI*)

1. For periodical articles later anthologized, *EGLI* may be considered a successor to *Poole's Index to Periodical Literature 1802-1907*] (S63); *The "A.L.A."* [American Library Association] *Index: An Index to General Literature*, 2nd ed. (Boston: Houghton, 1901) and its *Supplement, 1900-1910*, both with a cumulated author index by C. Edward Wall (1972); *The Nineteenth Century Readers' Guide* (S54); *The Wellesley Index* (S66); and *Literary Writings in America* (S60). Also see the *MLA International Bibliography* (M7), *Humanities Index* (S57), which analyzes the contents of modern British and North American scholarly journals; the *British Humanities Index* (S53), which analyzes additional British journals; the *Index to American Little Magazines* (S55); the *Index to Commonwealth Little Magazines* (S56); the *Index to Little Magazines* (S58); and Sader's *Comprehensive Index to English-Language Little Magazines* (S64). The major newspaper indexes are *Palmer's Index to the [London] Times Newspaper* and *The Times Index* (S62); and *The New York Times Index* and its valuable adjunct, *The Personal Name Index* (S61).

   For indexes to criticism, see checklist entry (M20,n.1) and *Cumulated Dramatic Index 1909-1949*, 2 vols. (Boston: Hall, 1965), extended through 1953 in *Bulletin of Bibliography*. For biography and bibliography, see *Biography Index* (S30) and *Bibliographic Index* (M18).

   Some other important indexes for locating primary sources include the following:

Columbia Granger's Index to Poetry. Ed. Edith P. Hazen and Deborah J. Fryer. 10th ed. New York: Columbia UP, 1994.

Connor, Billie M., and Helene G. Mochedlover. *Ottemiller's Index to Plays in Collections: An Author and Title Index to Plays Appearing in Collections Published between 1900 and 1985*. 7th ed. Metuchen, NJ: Scarecrow, 1988.

Play Index. New York: Wilson, 1953-. [Coverage goes back to 1949.]

Samples, Gordon. *The Drama Scholars' Index to Plays and Filmscripts: A Guide to Plays and Filmscripts in Selected Anthol-*

ogies, Series, and Periodicals. 3 vols. Metuchen, NJ: Scarecrow, 1974-86.

Short Story Index: An Index to Stories in Collections and Periodicals. New York: Wilson, 1953-. [Conveniently cumulated in *Short Story Index: Collections Indexed 1900-1978*.]

2. Periodical citations refer to the original publication source of an essay later included in a book. For earlier anthologies, use *EGLI* in conjunction with *Essay and General Literature Index: Works Indexed 1900-1969* (New York: Wilson, 1972).
3. For collections of miscellaneous essays by a single author, *EGLI* lists all the essays under the author's name, followed by the title of the book. The word "Contents" heads the lists of essays cited.

M28. *Book Review Index*. New York: Gale, 1965-.

Reviewers usually perform three functions: description, interpretation, and evaluation. Thus a particular review may serve as an introduction to a book, and a census of reviews may serve as an indicator of that book's reception by the author's contemporaries. Reviews in literary periodicals can make or break the reputations of authors. Reviews in scholarly journals are especially important as guides to the accuracy, thoroughness, and depth of secondary studies. *Book Review Index*, covering most fields, is current, easy to use, and on-line.

Contents:

1. Lists reviews in all subject areas in more than six hundred varied publications—books, library journals, general-interest periodicals, and scholarly/literary periodicals.[1]
2. Quarterly, cumulated annually.[2] Otherwise noncumulative aside from a cumulation for 1969-79.
3. Subtitles of works reviewed usually omitted.

4. Locates reviews of forthcoming books and periodicals,[3] citing periodical title, volume number, date or issue number, and pages on which the review appears.
5. Reviews new editions of older books.[4]
6. Minimum length of work reviewed must be fifty pages except for poetry and children's books.[5]
7. Unannotated but approximate word count of the review furnished, e.g., [1-50], [51-250], [501+].

Arrangement:

1. Publications indexed
   a. On cover endpapers: arranged by abbreviations of periodicals containing the reviews.
   b. Within introductory material: this section includes only frequency of publication and addresses.
2. Entries by author's/editor's name (by title if no primary author),[6] then alphabetically by title, and within the title listing, alphabetically by periodical abbreviation.
3. Identification of abbreviations of months and seasons on back cover endpaper.
4. Title index at back contains no publication information.

Review Questions:

1. Does *BRI* indicate the length of reviews?
2. How frequently does *BRI* appear?
3. Are reviewers' names given?
4. Where can you find periodical addresses?
5. For which of the following would you expect to find review citations in *BRI*?
   a. the audio version of Garrison Keillor's *The Book of Guys*?
   b. an Amanda Cross mystery?
   c. a 1962 study of Catholic doctrine?
   d. a short story from the *New Yorker*?
   e. *Religious Rite and Ceremony in Milton's Poetry*?
   f. *Peterson's Grants for Graduate Students 1989-90*?
   g. a French edition of Mozart librettos?
   h. *Gestaltung and Gestalten in modernen Drama* (1968)?

   i. a French translation of Nabokov's *Lolita*?
   j. a recent review in *Mother Jones* of a book entitled *Economics in an African Society*?
   k. *The Peter Pan Chronicles*?
6. Which of these would *BRI* include?
   a. a review you read in the *Los Angeles Times*?
   b. the place of publication for journals cited?
   c. the length of the review?
   d. the year in which the review appeared in a journal?
   e. annotation following the review citation?
   f. review citations for the same book in more than one annual volume of *BRI*?
   g. a high level of scholarly reviewing?
7. Could you locate a review in *BRI* if you knew only the title of the book?

Research Problems:

1. Provide the full titles of the periodicals that printed pre-publication reviews of *Vested Interests: Cross-Dressing and Cultural Anxiety* (1992).
2. For which of historian Fernand Braudel's books are reviews located in the 1985 *BRI* cumulation? In the 1994 cumulation?
3. In which *BRI* cumulation are reviews for Coppélia Kahn's *Man's Estate: Masculine Identity in Shakespeare* (1981) first listed in *BRI*? In which cumulation is the last one entered? Cite the reviews, explaining all abbreviations.
4. Where was the first issue of *City Lights Review: A Literary and Political Journal* reviewed in 1989? Cite full publication information, explaining all abbreviations.
5. Provide full information on *The Observer*'s 1993 review of Derek Jacobi's audio version of Homer's *Iliad*. Include the address of *The Observer*.
6. Cite reviews of Kafka's *Letters to Friends, Family, and Editors* listed in the 1977 *BRI* cumulation. Cite a review of J. Hibberd's *Kafka in Context*.

Notes (*BRI*)

1. *Book Review Index* is the best substitute for the more specialized *Index to Book Reviews in the Humanities*, which began publication in 1960 and was recently discontinued. (*IBRH* is now useful as a retrospective source for the past few decades.) Many nineteenth- and twentieth-century reiews are located in *Combined Retrospective Index to Book Reviews in Humanities Journals, 1802-1974*, 10 vols. (Woodbridge, CT: Research Publications, 1982-84). Nineteenth-century book reviews can be found in *Poole's Index* (S63), *Nineteenth Century Reader's Guide* (S54), *The Wellesley Index* (S66), and *Literary Writings in America* (S60). For the Romantic period, see William S. Ward, comp., *Literary Reviews in British Periodicals 1789-1797: A Bibliography: With a Supplementary List of General (Non-Review) Articles on Literary Subjects*, 2 vols. (New York: Garland, 1979); under the same title, different dates, are Ward's bibliographies for 1798-1826.
   An alternative to *BRI* for twentieth-century reviews is *Book Review Digest* (S52), which reprints excerpts from reviews and provides a word count. Reviews are also listed in *Arts and Humanities Citation Index* (S51), Sader's *Comprehensive Index to English-Language Little Magazines* (S64), *Index to Commonwealth Little Magazines* (S56), and *Index to Little Magazines* (S58). For reviews of scholarly/critical works, also see the *Annual Bibliography of English Language and Literature* (S35). For reviews of books too recent to have been indexed, consult the *New York Times Book Review* and the *Times Literary Supplement* (published by the London *Times*).
2. Since reviews often appear quite belatedly in scholarly journals, you should examine a number of volumes of *BRI*.
3. Reviews of periodicals or newspapers are designated by "p," of reference books by "r."
4. However, *BRI* omits the name of the editor, translator, or publisher unless more than one new edition is listed; thus the 1994 cumulation cites reviews of Swift's *Gulliver's Travels* but provides no further information about the edition.
5. *BRI* indicates whether a book is for children or adolescents. Also see *Children's Book Review Index* (S90) and *Children's Literature Review* (S90). Other *BRI* codes include an *R* before the page

number signifying a Roman numeral in the periodical, a * indicating the review's nonsequential pagination, and a + indicating that the review continues on succeeding pages.

6. Among *BRI*'s shortcomings are the omission of entries for co-authors, co-editors, and reviewers. (Reviewers' names are provided only in *BRI*'s first three cumulations, 1965-68, otherwise distinguished by being unpaginated.)

M29. *Books in Print 1995-96*. 9 vols. New York: Bowker, 1995. (Originated in 1948 as *An Author-Title-Series Index to the Publishers' Trade List Annual*.)[1]

Subject Guide to Books in Print, 1957-. 5 vols, 1995.

Books in Print Supplement, 1972-. 3 vols., 1996.

BIP may be regarded as one form of the current American national bibliogrphy; from 1948 on, it has provided an annual listing of most of the books published and/or distributed in the United States.[2] In consequence, *BIP* can be found in virtually all bookstores and libraries, however small. Information regarding the price of various editions of a book is particularly useful to instructors choosing required texts for their students.[3] Volumes 1 through 4 of *BIP* are an author index; volumes 5 through 8, a title index. Volume 9 is devoted to information about publishers and distributors.

The following description, review questions, and research problems are based on *BIP*, its *Subject Guide*, and *Supplement*, all for 1995-96.[4]

Contents (*BIP*):

1. Almost all hardcover and most paperbound books in print; includes trade books, textbooks, and juveniles.[5]
2. Books forthcoming within the year.[6]
3. Full ordering information: may include author (or editor, compiler, translator), title, original title, number of volumes, volume number, edition, whether reprinted, LC number and ISBN

(International Standard Book Number), subject information, number of pages, grade range, whether illustrated, type of binding, price, imprint, publisher, date, series, and language.
4. Cross-reference from co-authors, co-editors, and various forms of an author's name.

Arrangement (BIP):

1. [Vol. 1] How to Use *BIP* (see for M', Mc, Mac entries and any difficulties encountered with initials or abbreviations).[7]
2. [Vol. 1] Key to basic abbreviations.
3. Vols. 1-4, alphabetically arranged author index.
4. Vols. 5-8, alphabetically arranged title index.
5. Publishers' and distributors' abbreviations, addresses, toll-free phone and fax numbers, list of new publishers, and the like.

Contents and Arrangement (Subject Guide to BIP):

1. All books in print (including biographical and historical fiction) suitable for entry under a subject heading, generally LC; single works of fiction, poetry, and drama that do not lend themselves to a subject approach should be looked up in *BIP*.
2. Entries duplicate those in *BIP*.
3. [Vol. 1] front, directions for use and key to abbreviations.
4. [Vols. 1-4] Index proper.

Contents and Arrangement (Supplement):

1. An annual issued six months after *BIP*.
2. Updates with regard to prices, publication dates, ISBN and LC numbers, and availability.
3. Three separate indexes: vol. 1, authors;[8] vol. 2, titles A-M; vol. 3, Titles N-Z, subjects, and publishers.

Review Questions:

1. Are periodicals entered in *BIP* or in the *Subject Guide*?

2. Does *BIP* list every published paperbound book?
3. What information does *BIP* provide that is especially useful for instructors choosing an edition of a classic for class use?
4. Could you learn from *BIP* whether a work was available in the 1950s?
5. If a work is not currently in print, where would you try to locate it?
6. Which volumes of *BIP* are the author index?
7. For books dealing with Chaucer's sources, would you look in volumes 1-8 of *BIP* or in the *Subject Guide to BIP*?
8. When is the *Supplement* issued? How is it indexed? When should you consult it?

Research Problems:

1. Which of these books were in print in 1995-96: A. C. Bradley's *Shakespearean Tragedy*, G. B. Harrison's *Profession of English*, Sinclair Lewis's *Ann Vickers*, E. M. W. Tillyard's *Shakespeare's History Plays*? Which does *BIP* list as available in paperback?
2. Name a paperbound collection of nineteenth-century English plays in print in 1995-96.
3. Name a two-volume annotated bibliography published in 1973-83 of literary criticism about Thomas Hardy. Of what series is this bibliography a part? Cite the publisher and the address.
4. In 1995-96 what was the list price of Janis Lull's chronology of the metaphysical poets? What other work of hers is listed?
5. Who published the least expensive edition of Mary Stewart's *The Hollow Hills*, available in 1995-96? When was the sequel, *The Last Enchantment*, published by that press in its current edition? What is special about Thorndike's edition of Stewart's *The Stormy Petrel*?
6. State the editor and title of a collection of English political ballads and songs available in 1995-96. Who are the current publishers of both reprints?

Notes (*BIP*)

1. *The Publishers' Trade List Annual* (New York: Bowker, 1873), a yearly collection of American publishers' catalogs, may be used to discover what works are part of a publisher's series, since *BIP* is no longer a series index.
2. For the reference components of an American national bibliography from its beginnings to the present, see Evans's *American Bibliography* (M24), Sabin's *Bibliotheca Americana* (S48), and the *Cumulative Book Index* (S45).
3. Although publishers attempt to anticipate price changes (as well as books soon to be in print or out), Bowker's *BIP Supplement* should be consulted for interim changes.
4. All of these are available on CD-ROM and are updated more frequently than the printed volumes.
5. See front of vol. 1, Authors A-F, for exclusions. Note that Bowker publishes a *Children's Books in Print* (S80). Also see Whitaker's Books in Print (formerly *The Reference Catalogue of Current Literature* [1874-]), an annual five-volume, author-title-subject index, and *Paperbound Books in Print* (1955-), a more reliable source for current paperbacks than *BIP*.
6. A separate bimonthly publication, Bowker's *Forthcoming Books* (1966-), provides author-title indexes to all books scheduled to appear within the next five months.
7. Since variant forms of an author's name (e.g., Goethe/ von Goethe, E. M. W. Tillyard/ Eustace M. Tillyard) may not be filed adjacent to each other, always check variant forms when using the author index.
8. Because entries in the author index are truncated, page references to full entries in the title indexes are provided.

M30. *MLA Directory of Periodicals: A Guide to Journals and Series in Languages and Literatures*. New York: MLA, 1978/79-.

This "companion to the *MLA International Bibliography*" is the best source of information about journals and book series for scholarly and creative writers seeking the appropriate vehicles for their critical or scholarly essays, poetry, short fiction, bibliographies, and reviews. More than three thousand journals and book series on languages, literature, and folklore are described.[1] The 1996-1998 volume is described below.

Contents:

1. General information:[2] includes name of editor, submission address, date of periodical's origin, sponsoring organization, MLA (i.e., standard) acronym, and International Standard Serial Number.
2. Subscription information: frequency of publication, whether available in microform, circulation, subscription address, sometimes rates.
3. Advertising information: whether accepted.
4. Editorial information: the journal's or series' concerns and intended purpose, the language or languages accepted, whether it prints notes, reviews, and abstracts.
5. Submission requirements: Restrictions on contributors; length of articles, reviews, and notes; style manual to be followed; number of copies required for submission; any special format requirements (e.g., anonymous submission); policy on copyright ownership and return of rejected manuscripts; time before publication decision and between decision and publication; number of reviewers, number of articles, reviews, and notes respectively submitted per year and the number published.[3]

Arrangement:

1. Table of Contents and Guide for Users
2. Master List of Periodicals
3. Alphabetical numbered entries to which index citations refer.
4. Indexes to subjects, sponsoring organizations, editorial personnel, languages in which articles and monographs are published (other than English, German, French, Spanish, and Italian), and periodicals with author-anonymous submission policies.

Review Questions:

1. For what purposes would you use the *MLA Directory of Periodicals*?
2. How can you tell how good your chances are of having your work accepted?
3. For which of these would you expect to find entries: *Esquire, Modern Philology, Mark Twain Journal, La Revue des Lettres Moderne, Journal of Psychology, Research in Text Theory*?

Research Problems:

1. What journal does Bernard F. McTigue edit? When did it originate? What special requirements are stipulated?
2. Which German journal might be interested in your article on Shaw's response to Mozart's *Don Giovanni*?
3. What review is most likely to be interested in your article on Garcia Lorca? Who sponsors the review? What is its circulation? How many copies of your manuscript are required? How does the submission-acceptance ratio for articles compare with that of other journals?
4. What restrictions are placed on contributors to the *CEA Critic*? Which style guide must be followed? What are the minimum and maximum length of articles?
5. How many book series does Twayne publish? What restrictions on contributors and special requirements are stipulated for Twayne's World Authors Series?
6. Whose work is welcomed by *Comitatus*? What kinds of studies are invited? What is the desired length of articles? Of notes?

Notes (*MLADP*)

1. Also see *Ulrich's International Periodicals Directory* (S65) and *The Standard Periodical Directory* (New York: Oxbridge, 1965-), especially under the heading Poetry and Creative Writing. Both of these reference works are not limited to literature and languages but are instead comprehensive. Information on placing

creative work can be found in such aids as the *Directory of Literary Magazines*, 1984-, *Poet's Market*, 1985-, *Writer's Digest*, 1920-, and *Writer's Market*, 1922-. Note that there is also an *MLA Directory of Scholarly Presses in Language and Literature*, ed. James L. Harner (New York: MLA, 1991).

2. Because of the inevitable time lag (i.e., compilation of the 1996-1998 edition would have ended for the most part in 1995), some information may not be current; editors change jobs, journals or editorial policies are discontinued, and submission-acceptance ratios are apt to become more challenging.
3. It is always advisable to look at a few issues of a likely journal before submitting your work.

CHAPTER 5

SOME AUXILIARY TOOLS

M31. *Key Sources in Comparative and World Literature*

M32. Variorum: *The Variorum Edition of the Plays of W. B. Yeats*

M33. Concordance: *Concordance to the Plays of W. B. Yeats*

M34. Bartlett's *Familiar Quotations*

M35. *New Moulton's Library of Literary Criticism* and *The Critical Perspective*

M36. *The New Encyclopaedia Britannica* and *Britannica Book of the Year*

Chapter 5 introduces a number of miscellaneous works, all of importance to students of literature. *Key Sources in Comparative and World Literature* is part bibliography, part guide to many of the world's literatures. A variorum edition presents all the extant versions of a particular work and often provides a compendium of criticism on that work as well. A concordance may be regarded as an index to the words an author uses. Bartlett's, though chronologically arranged, is actually an index of famous quotations. *The New Moulton's Library of Literary*

Criticism and its predecessors and spin-offs serve both as surveys and indexes to important interpretations of literature. *Britannica*, still the outstanding multivolumed general encyclopedia, may perhaps best be used as an initial source for extraliterary information.

M31. Thompson, George A., Jr. *Key Sources in Comparative and World Literature.* New York: Ungar, 1982.

Thompson's useful compilation is aimed primarily at beginning graduate students rather than specialists. Attempting to cover reference works on much of the world's writings in less than four hundred pages, Thompson is perforce highly selective. *Key Sources* is most successful in its treatment of individual literatures rather than comparative literature. Of the former, the most space is devoted to Western literatures. Although Thompson lists many different kinds of research materials, bibliographies predominate.

Contents:

1. Comparative, general, and international literatures.
2. The influence of classical literature on later works.
3. Medieval and modern Greek and Latin literature.
4. American, Spanish-American,[1] European, and Asian literatures.
5. World literature in English—the longest chapter.
6. Related fields in the arts and humanities.
7. Bibliographies of translations into English, themes, genres, periods, and movements.
8. Bibliographies and concordances for better-known authors.[2]
9. Guides, handbooks, encyclopedias, literary histories, reviews of research, dissertations, biographies, indexes.[3]
10. Descriptive, occasionally evaluative annotations in English.
11. Reviews selectively located.

Arrangement:

1. Overall table of contents.
2. Explanation of reference terms on pp. x-xi of the Introduction.

3. Periodical abbreviations explained at front, pp. xiii-xv.
4. At the beginning of each chapter, a detailed outline of its contents with item numbers.
5. Chapter numbers precede item numbers, e.g., 6/23, represents the twenty-third entry in chapter 6.
6. Within the chapters, works are ordered according to usefulness, i.e., from the general to the specific.
7. Three indexes: a name index, a selective index of titles and institutions, and a subject index.

Review Questions:

1. For which of the following would you expect to find entries: African literature, a German-language dictionary of religion, an index that includes criticism of Islamic literature, a Norwegian-language history of English literature, a bibliography of criticism on Katherine Anne Porter, a bibliography on Shakespeare's use of the classics, a handbook on folk epics throughout the world, a literary history of Spain written in English, a history of picaresque literature written in Spanish?
2. What does 8/163 signify?

Research Problems:

1. Who are the individual authors Thompson lists under twentieth-century Russian literature? Where is the concordance to Mandelstam reviewed? Cite a bibliography of Polish plays that have been translated into English.
2. Cite a history of Israeli literature. In what language are quotations given?
3. Cite a multi-language bibliography on French structuralism. Which theorists are discussed? What work is the bibliography intended to supplement?
4. Cite a study of European scholarship on courtly love. Which part deals with theories of origin? In what journal is the study called "immensely helpful"? (Explain abbreviations.)
5. Cite two ongoing serial bibliographies of Old English literature and an annual review of Old English research. In which periodicals are these bibliographies published?

6. What specific themes does Thompson list under General and International Literature? Where has the English-language work on Utopian writings been reviewed? Explain abbreviations.

Notes (Thompson)

1. Spanish-American literatures are not listed individually by country, but instead are treated monolithically.
2. As an example, for twentieth-century American literature only Eliot, Faulkner, and Hemingway are singled out.
3. Also see all supplementary entries under the heading Comparative and World Literature.

M32. *The Variorum Edition of the Plays of W. B. Yeats*. Ed. Russell K. Alspach. New York: Macmillan, 1966.

Alspach's work is an example of the modern variorum edition. Although Alspach deals with one genre within the author's canon, a variorum editor may treat only a single work or may treat an author's entire canon. The value of the modern variorum is twofold: Presenting variant versions both reveals the development of a work and also allows the reader to choose among alternate readings where the writer's final choice is uncertain. Older variorum editions contain not only variant readings but line-by-line critical annotations by famous commentators; see, for example, *A New Variorum Edition of Shakespeare*, ed. Horace Howard Furness (Philadelphia: Lippincott, 1871-), now in 23 volumes with continuing bibliographical supplements issued under the auspices of the Modern Language Association of America.

Contents:

1. Basic text of the plays: based on the London Macmillan edition of *The Collected Plays of W. B. Yeats* (1952); numbered lines.
2. List of all significant printings of the plays.

3. Line-by-line entering of all variant versions (changes, additions, and deletions in words and punctuation), citing the printings in which the variants occur.
4. Reprinting of the original version of plays revised so drastically as to preclude intelligible collation with later versions.
5. Yeats's prefaces, dedications, and notes to the plays collated with their variant versions.

Arrangement:

1. Table of Contents, pp. xvii-xviii.
2. Bibliography, pp. xix-xxiv: the editions collated listed chronologically and numbered for cross-reference to the variant readings.
3. The Collations, p. xxv: explanation of symbols, abbreviations, and method used.
4. The plays; the page is divided by a horizontal line with the basic text printed above the line, the variants below; when Alspach reprints the original version of a play, it appears on the verso (left-hand) page only.
5. Yeats's notes to a particular play printed at the end of that play; cross-references to other notes.
6. Appendix I: Yeats's general notes.
7. Appendix II: Yeats's Prefaces and Dedications, primarily from the plays.
8. Appendix III: Dates, Places of Performance, and Casts of Characters of First Productions.
9. Index, Part I; alphabetical list of characters citing the play in which the character appears and the line in both the basic text and the variants where s/he first speaks. Part II, General Index.

Review Questions:

1. What is the difference between a modern variorum edition and an older one like Furness's *New Variorum Edition of Shakespeare*?
2. Why is a variorum edition valuable to critics?
3. Why are the lines of the variorum text numbered?
4. How is the basic text separated from the variant readings?
5. How do you use Alspach's bibliography?

Research Problems:

1. Which of the following plays did Yeats revise the most and which the least: *Sophocles' King Oedipus: A Version for the Modern State*; *The Unicorn from the Stars*; *The Countess Cathleen*? What original production conditions influenced Yeats's purpose and style in his *King Oedipus*?
2. What does Yeats have to say about the Elizabethan stage in contrast to the modern theater?
3. In which version of Yeats's *On Baile's Strand* are these lines found?

   197. I think that a fierce woman's better, a woman
   198. That breaks away when you have thought her won,
   199. For I'd be fed and hungry at one time.

   Does Yeats keep this passage in any later versions of the play? How do you know?
4. Name the play in which each character appears and the line, in both the basic text and the variants, where the character first speaks: Naoisi, Judas, The Morrigu.
5. In which printing of *The Countess Cathleen* is the dedication to Maud Gonne lacking? In which printings of *On Baile's Strand* are there stage directions after line 60?
6. Where and when was *The Player Queen* first produced? Who played Nona? In what magazine was the play first printed?

M33. *A Concordance to the Plays of W. B. Yeats*. Ed. Eric Domville. 2 vols. Ithaca: Cornell University Press, 1972.

Domville's work is an example of a computer-produced concordance.[1] A concordance is an alphabetical index of all words used in the work or works treated, citing the line in which they occur. A concordance can be based on a single work, e.g., *Byron's Don Juan*, ed. Charles W. Hagelman, Jr. and Robert J. Barnes (Ithaca: Cornell University Press, 1967); on one or more genres within an author's canon, as is the work at hand; or on an author's entire literary output, e.g., *A Concordance to the Writings of William Blake*, ed. David V. Erdman, 2 vols. (Ithaca: Cornell University Press, 1967). The most frequent uses of a concordance are to determine the author's vocabulary, to discover the various senses in which s/he uses a word, to discover words characteristic of the author's style, to find a work's imagery patterns as reflected in the high frequency of particular words, and to help locate a partly forgotten passage.

Prior to 1955, concordances were prepared manually; in consequence, listed words are usually quoted in a lengthier and more intelligible context. See, for example, *A Concordance to the Poems of Edmund Spenser*, ed. Charles Grosvenor Osgood (1915; rpt. Gloucester, MA: Peter Smith, 1963).

Contents:

1. All the words in the plays and in significant variant lines, cited in the context of the line; the concordance is based upon Alspach's *Variorum Edition of the Plays* (M32).
2. Excludes names of speakers, stage directions, and such insignificant words as *a, am, an*, etc.
3. Frequency count of words entered.

Arrangement:

1. Preface: list of omitted words, 1: x; explanation of line numbering, 1: xi-xii; list of abbreviations, 1: xiii-xiv; explanation of variant entries, I-xiv-xv.
2. Alphabetical entries: the concordance proper.
3. Appendix: Index of words in order of frequency, 2: 1533-58; the list is headed by words used most frequently and ends with words used only once.

Review Questions:

1. Specify some of the uses of a concordance.
2. Why is it important to know what text the concordance is based upon?
3. What main classes of words does Domville omit from his concordance?
4. What does the Appendix contain?

Research Problems:

Concordance and *Variorum*

1. This line begins the last song of one of Yeats's plays: "The wind blows out of the gates of the day. . . ." Quote the rest of the song. In what play does it appear?
2. In which of his plays does Yeats use the word "dreamless"? Quote the intelligible context (two lines or more) in which this word occurs.
3. In which of his plays does Yeats use the word "dawn-blenched"? Quote the quatrain in which it appears.

Concordance

4. Note the frequencies of the following words in Yeats's plays: old 527, God 391, heart 261, dead 225, death 185. Are these high-, middle-, or low-frequency words? What kinds of words have a frequency of more than 1,000?
5. In which of his plays does Yeats refer to Alexandria? To Arcadia? To Cambridge?
6. Which of these words does Yeats use most frequently: beauteous, beauties, beautiful, beauty? In which of his plays does he use the word "beauty" most frequently?

Notes (*Concordance*)

1. How computers produce concordances is described in Robert L. Oakman, *Computer Methods for Literary Research* (S15).

M34. Bartlett, John. *Familiar Quotations: A Collection of Passages, Phrases and Proverbs Traced to Their Sources in Ancient and Modern Literature.* 16th ed. Ed. Justin Kaplan. Boston: Little, Brown, 1992.

Bartlett's is the standard compendium, useful for locating the source of quotations and for verifying their wording. It is comprehensive, accurate, and conveniently arranged. The work proper is ordered chronologically; the two indexes provide an author-subject (i.e., keyword) approach.

Contents:

1. International in scope.
2. From 3500 B.C. (ancient Egypt).
3. Poetry and prose[1]—includes song lyrics and movies.
4. Anonymous quotations as well as those by known authors.
5. For known authors, birth and death dates are given.
6. Works from which quotations are taken are dated.
7. Exact location of each quotation is cited (e.g., chapter and verse; act, scene, line).
8. For non-English quotations, the original wording is given in a footnote if the language is familiar.

Arrangement:

1. Introductory user's guide, pp. xii-xiv.
2. Alphabetical index of authors with their dates, pp. xv-lvi.
3. Chronological entries.
4. Anonymous quotations arranged chronologically beginning p. 775; see p. 132 for early anonymous quotations.[2]
5. Footnotes to entries: similar thoughts expressed by other writers, cross-references, history of sources, and other annotations.
6. Alphabetical index by keywords, p. [939] ff: unusually full; several keywords for each quotation.
7. The first index number is the page; the quotation's number follows the colon. A footnote is indicated by "n."

Review Questions:

1. How extensive is Bartlett's coverage?
2. According to what principle are the main entries arranged?
3. According to what principle are the indexes arranged?
4. How do you use a keyword index?

Research Problems:

1. Identify the exact source of both quotations:
   a. "The almond tree shall flourish, and the grasshopper shall be a burden, and desire shall fail; because man goeth to his long home, and the mourners go about the streets. . . ."
   b. "The stroke of death is as a lover's pinch, / Which hurts, and is desir'd."
2. What did Charles Lamb have to say about mountains? Edna St. Vincent Millay about burning the candle at both ends? Swift about satire? (Cite sources.)
3. What famous remarks have been attributed to Alexander the Great?
4. Quote the poem that begins "Even such is time. . . ." Who wrote it and where was it found?
5. What was Thomas à Kempis's Latin for "So passes away the glory of this world"? Of what ceremony are these words a part?
6. Who dubbed Shakespeare the "sweet swan of Avon"? Cite the author and title of the work in which these lines appear:
   O O O O that Shakespeherian Rag—
   It's so elegant
   So intelligent.

Notes (Bartlett's)

1. More complete coverage of British quotations, especially quotations from British poetry, can be found in *The Oxford Dictionary of Quotations*, ed. Angela Partington, 4th ed. (Oxford: Oxford UP, 1992).

   Another useful work is *Magill's Quotations in Context*, ed. Frank N. Magill (New York: Harper, 1965), and its supplementary *Second Series* (1969); Magill presents the quotation in a context of from approximately seven to fifteen lines, provides a brief (about two hundred words) plot summary or description of the work in which the quotation appears, and explains the relevance of the quotation to the larger context. Also see *Brewer's Dictionary of Phrase and Fable* (S12) and *The Oxford Dictionary of English Proverbs* (S17).

2. Anonymous quotations are subdivided. See Index of Authors under Anonymous for these subdivisions, e.g., African, ballad, etc.

M35. *The New Moulton's Library of Literary Criticism: Pre-Twentieth-Century Criticism of British and American Literature to 1904.* Ed. Harold Bloom. 11 vols. The Chelsea House Library of Literary Criticism. New York: Chelsea House, 1985-90. [Vol. 11 is the index.]

The Critical Perspective: Twentieth-Century Criticism of British and American Literature to 1904. Ed. Harold Bloom. 11 vols. The Chelsea House Library of Literary Criticism. New York: Chelsea House, 1985-89.

These compilations of critical quotations are valuable not only in themselves but also as an index to literary criticism. Excerpted works are fully documented and are therefore easy to locate. Charles Wells Moulton's original eight-volume work, now revised and expanded under the general editorship of Bloom, himself an eminent critic, served as the model for the current survey of pre-twentieth century opinions about past and contemporary literature.

The New Moulton's is described below in detail; significant differences between this work and its sequel, *The Critical Perspective,* are noted under the latter.

Contents (*The New Moulton's*, vols. 1-10):

1. Extracts from selected critical writings (laudatory poems, journals, and book-length histories, etc.) about English and American authors by critics of all nationalities.
2. Critical essays.
3. Coverage of authors and their critics from the eighth century A.D. through the Edwardian period.[1]
4. Brief biographical sketches of the authors or, for older works, the history of the manuscript.
5. Some illustrations.

Arrangement:

1. Table of Contents: each volume has its own table of contents and list of illustrations at the front.
2. Entries arranged chronologically by period and author's death dates (i.e., vol. 1 covers the medieval and early Renaissance periods; it begins with *Beowulf* and ends with Richard Hakluyt [d. 1616]).
3. Each main entry contains a biographical sketch, followed by personal criticism, general criticism, and criticism of individual works; criticism is presented chronologically.
4. Exact source references cited.

Vol. 11, *Bibliographical Supplement and Index*:

1. Bibliographies of primary authors.
2. Index to those bibliographies.
3. Chronological listing of the contents of the 10-volume series.
4. Index to primary authors within the series.
5. Index to critics cited within the series.

Contents and Arrangement (*The Critical Perspective*):

1. Twentieth-century criticism through the 1980s.
2. Long excerpts or complete essays with endnotes.[2]
3. Wide-ranging approaches (e.g., new critical to post-structuralist).
4. Some minor authors who appeared in *The New Moulton's* are omitted here.
5. Volume 11 is the *Bibliographical Supplement and Index*; it follows the same arrangement as volume 11 of *The New Moulton's.*

Review Questions:

1. In which work can you find twentieth-century criticism of pre-twentieth century authors?
2. Where is the index to *The Critical Perspective*? How is it arranged?

3. In which work can you find twentieth-century criticism of American authors?
4. Aside from critical excerpts, what information can be found in *The New Moulton's*?
5. Why is it useful to have critical excerpts entered chronologically?

Research Problems:

1. Who wrote the 1980s biographical discussion of Mary Wollstonecraft? To what does she attribute distortions of Wollstonecraft's biography? To what does she attribute Wollstonecraft's craving "from her youth a permanent attachment to another female"? How does Virginia Woolf explain Wollstonecraft's death?
2. To which of Hardy's novels does William Dean Howells compare Stephen Crane's *Maggie*? Quote Crane's statement to Willa Cather about his writing *The Red Badge of Courage* in nine days.
3. About whom did each of these creative writers write literary criticism: Brian Aldiss, Kingsley Amis, W. H. Auden, Jorge Luis Borges, Anthony Burgess, and G. K. Chesterton?
4. Whose criticism (1952) of Donne's "divine poems" is excerpted in *The Critical Perspective*? According to that critic, what step had Donne taken that created a need, perhaps reflected in the lines "for Oh, to some / Not to be Martyrs, is a martyrdome"?
5. How does Kerry McSweeney explain the neglect of George Eliot's *Middlemarch* in the 1920s and 1930s?
6. How many collections of the letters of Lady Mary Wortley Montagu were published in her lifetime? How many collections of the letters of Lord Chesterfield were published in his lifetime?

Notes (*New Moulton's* and *Critical Perspective*)

1. Similar coverage of twentieth-century authors can be found in *Twentieth-Century British Literature*, ed. Harold Bloom, 6 vols., The Chelsea House Library of Literary Criticism (N.Y.: Chelsea House, 1985-87); and *Twentieth-Century American Literature*, ed. Harold Bloom, 8 vols., The Chelsea House Library of Literary Criticism (N.Y.: Chelsea House, 1985-88). Although not Chelsea publications, under the title, subtitle, or series title *A Library of*

Literary Criticism are works on modern Commonwealth, French, German, Latin American, romance, and Slavic literatures, on modern dramatists, and on modern black writers.

Also see *Contemporary Literary Criticism* (M16, n.4), its companion work *Twentieth-Century Literary Criticism* (M16, n.5), and *Magill's Bibliography of Literary Criticism* (M20, n.1).

2. These endnotes can serve you as a finding list or bibliography.

M36. *The New Encyclopaedia Britannica.* 15th ed. 32 vols. Chicago: Encyclopaedia Britannica, 1974. [1995 printing]

Britannica Book of the Year [1938-].

What is new about Britannica's fifteenth edition—*The New Encyclopaedia Britannica*—is its tripartite format. The twelve-volume *Micropaedia* serves as a source of capsule information. The seventeen-volume *Macropaedia* provides extensive studies, and the single-volume *Propaedia* is a topical table of contents.[1] (Two index volumes, 31 and 32, complete the set.) The format of *Britannica* reflects the editors' attempt to provide 1) a sense of a topic's place within the framework of human knowledge, 2) an in-depth study of the topic, and 3) a brief "ready reference" summary of that topic.

Begin by consulting the index volumes, where you will find references to your subject in the *Micropaedia* and/or *Macropaedia.* You may wish to refer to the *Propaedia*'s outline of knowledge to better understand your subject's place in the grand scheme of things and to find related subjects for further reading. For students of literature *Britannica* is likely to be most useful as an introduction to extraliterary subjects.[2]

Current events are treated in the *Britannica Book of the Year*, an ongoing publication.[3] The 1994 volume of *Britannica Book of the Year* is described below as an example of the yearbook's present format.

Contents (*Micropaedia*, vols. 1-12):

1. "Ready-reference" articles of 750 words or less, some by well-known specialists (Antonia Fraser on Mary Queen of Scots, Arthur Mizener on F. Scott Fitzgerald).[4]
2. Synopses of *Macropaedia* major articles.
3. Numerous maps, illustrations, and statistical charts in the text.
4. Some bibliography.

Arrangement:

1. Alphabetically arranged, with substantives first, e.g., the Tower of London is found under London, Tower of.
2. Cross-references to other articles: indicated by *see, see also, q.v.* (*quod vide*=which see), *q.q.v.* (plural form), or RELATED ENTRIES.
3. List of *Micropaedia* abbreviations at end of each volume.

Contents (*Macropaedia*, vols. 13-29):

1. Signed major articles on all subjects by authorities in their fields, e.g., Arnold Toynbee on Time.
2. Illustrations and maps in the text.
3. Extensive classified and evaluative bibliographies appended to articles.

Arrangement:

1. Table of Contents for each volume.
2. Alphabetically arranged.
3. Many of the lengthier articles both introduced and outlined.
4. Both marginal subheadings and boldface subheadings within the text.

Contents and Arrangement (*Propaedia*, vol. 30):

1. How to Use the *Propaedia*, p. 4.
2. Table of Contents (to the *Propaedia* only), pp. 9-15.
3. The outline proper divided into ten parts:

a. matter and energy
b. the earth
c. life on earth
d. human life
e. human society
f. art
g. technology
h. religion
i. the history of mankind
j. the branches of knowledge

4. Authoritative introductory essays to each part; for example, Mark Van Doren introduces The World of Art.[5]
5. Further analytical breakdown into divisions and sections of learning, each preceded by an explanatory headnote, then final subdivision into separate subjects.
6. Identification by initials of authors of *Britannica* articles, pp. 521-65: includes institutional affiliation and major publications; pp. 656-67: identification by name; pp. 676-745: writers and advisers of *Micropaedia* articles.

Contents and Arrangement: *1994 Book of the Year*:

1. Contains articles on events of 1993.
2. Table of Contents lists feature articles, a chronology, "The Year in Review"; major revisions of a few *Macropaedia* articles from the previous year's printing; and "World Data," providing social, economic, and demographic statistics for the countries surveyed.
3. Under "The Year in Review" subjects are alphabetically arranged. Of special interest to literature students are "Biographies," "Obituaries" "Literature," and "Theatre."
4. Identification of contributors to this *Book of the Year* immediately preceding "World Data."
5. Cumulative index to articles in this *Book of the Year* and the ten previous ones at end of volume.

Review Questions:

1. Which part contains long articles? Which contains the topical table of contents or outline of knowledge? Which contains bibliographies?
2. Where can you discover who wrote a particular article?
3. Which are the famous older editions of *Britannica*?
4. Where can you learn about recently deceased writers? About the 1993 National Theatre season? Where can you find out how many teachers are involved in higher education in the United States and how this figure compares with that of other countries?

Research Problems:

Britannica, 15th and 11th editions

1. Whose folk beliefs were codified in the *Malleus maleficarum*? What is the English title of this work? Using the *Propaedia* outline at the beginning of Part 8, trace the relationship between the general topic of religion and witchcraft by noting the appropriate major analytical headings. Does the eleventh edition's discussion of the *Malleus* contain any surprising additional information about confessions extracted through torture?

Britannica Book of the Year 1994

2. What prizes were awarded to E. Annie Proulx for *The Shipping News*? To Barbara Kingsolver? For what book?
3. At what schools was Tony Kushner educated? Who will direct the film version of *Angels in America*? Describe some of the diverse characters who appear in *Angels*.

Britannica, 15th edition

4. Where is Culloden, and what are its associations with the Young Pretender? Whose grandson was Bonnie Prince Charlie? In the 1986 printing, the ultimate effect of the Forty-five Rebellion on the Highlands is described thus: the Highlands "became a part of the United Kingdom and knew peace" (29: 72)). In the 1995 printing, the author of the *Macropaedia* article on the United Kingdom talks about the "gradual" pacification of Scotland? To

what does he attribute pacification? How would you characterize the change in *Britannica*'s slant?

5. Under what other names is Nefertiti known? Where is her portrait bust kept? Who wrote the classic statement about Akhenaton at the turn of the twentieth century?
6. For what work is Adelbert von Chamisso best remembered? What is it about? What might it allegorize? Who set Chamisso's *Frauen-Liebe und Leben* to music?

Notes (*Britannica*)

1. *Micropaedia*, *Macropaedia*, and *Propaedia* are the editor's neologisms for little, great, and before[hand] learning.
2. *The New Columbia Encyclopedia*, ed. Barbara A. Chernow and George A. Vallasi, 5th ed. (New York: Columbia UP, 1993) is an excellent one-volume general encyclopedia. For major extra-literary research, you will want to consult such specialized encyclopedias as the *International Encyclopedia of the Social Sciences* (S75), *The Encyclopedia of Philosophy* (S67), *Encyclopaedia of Religion* (S68), *New Catholic Encyclopedia* (S73), *Encyclopedia Judaica* (S69), *Encyclopedia of World Art* (S70), and *The New Grove Dictionary of Music and Musicians* (S74). Also see the *Dictionary of the History of Ideas* (S24).
3. In fact, the entire encyclopedia is now available on CD-ROM and on-line, thus enhancing its currency.
4. If currency is not of the essence, the famous ninth (1875-89) and eleventh (1910-11) editions are of great value. (*Britannica* originated in the latter half of the eighteenth century.) Treatment of subjects in the humanities and history is frequently more detailed than in the latest edition, and among the contributors to these editions are writers who have themselves become subjects of research, such as Algernon Swinburne, William Morris, and Lord Macaulay.
5. Literature, as a particular art, occupies eight pages of Part VI. Outlined are theoretical aspects of literature, literature's relationship to the other arts, technical aspects, literary types, children's literature, folk and popular literatures, and the history of literature. There follows a list of articles on literature for further reading.

GENERAL REVIEW 3

1. Compile a list of major Russian poets born after 1920. Which of these were once married to one another?

2. Who wrote *Britannica*'s major article on Shakespeare? (Use the 15th edition.) Name the authors of the two standard multi-volumed works on the theater in Shakespeare's time.

3. What is the "Fitzgerald stanza"? Quote one. How did Fitzgerald's best-known work affect his era? (This question has to do with the British poet, not the American fiction writer.)

4. Give the history of the poem, the first stanza of which appears below:

   Stay with me God. The night is dark,
   The night is cold: my litttle spark
   Of courage dies. The night is long;
   Be with me, God, and make me strong.

5. What nineteenth-century English poet wrote a play about Harold, the last of the Saxon kings? Which two other English historical figures did he use as the subjects of plays?

6. Using a specialized serial bibliography, determine what are the "harmonies" of Lawrence Danson's *The Harmonies of "The Merchant of Venice"* (1978)? Who finds Danson's book "fair-minded and central"?

7. Locate the collection in which D. H. Lawrence's essay "State of Funk," written prior to 1931, appears. Cite author, title of book, publisher, and date.

8. Determine whether "air" is one of Yeats's characteristic words by noting in how many of his plays he uses some form of "air." Is this number more or less than half of the plays he wrote? (Count A and B texts as one play.)

9. Frank Lloyd Wright was ostensibly the inspiration for the hero of which American novels?

10. Provide the title of a late-1980s reference guide compiled under the auspices of the American Library Association, addressing the subject of twentieth-century science fiction. About how many authors are treated? Who compiled a major bibliography on the early years of science fiction, listing more than three thousand stories?

11. List four collections of the letters of the poet William Morris (1834-96).

12. Who reviewed the March 1992 airing of David Thacker's television production of Ibsen's *A Doll's House* for *New York Magazine*? For the *New York Times*? For *Variety*?

13. In his 1896 essay on "The New Poetry," with what poet does George Saintsbury compare Keats? Which poet does Saintsbury regard as more "germinal"? Which poems are Keats's "twin peaks," according to Saintsbury?

14. What happens to the title character in the first play published in America?

15. What childhood incident made George Bernard Shaw aware that his father was an irresponsible drinker? Who is the biographer you are following?

16. In what work can you find a listing of Arthur Miller's short stories, radio plays, essays, and interviews through the mid-1960s? What other information does this work contain? Name the first full-length study of Norman Mailer. Cite an article by James Baldwin on Norman Mailer.

17. When was Richard Henry Dana Jr.'s *An Autobiographical Sketch* (1815-42) first published in its entirety? How large was the edition? Where can a copy be seen?

18. Quote the epigraph Yeats wrote to *Cathleen ni Houlihan*. In which edition can it be found? In his letter to Lady Gregory (February 1903), what incident does Yeats recount as the inspiration for this play?

19. Cite an essay published in 1984 on postmodernist literary theory that uses Roland Barthes's work as an example. Give full publication information.

20. What special award did South African Archbishop Desmond Tutu receive in 1984? How many honorary degrees does he hold? Which of Rose Tremain's novels won the *Sunday Express* Book of the Year Award? What society admitted her as a Fellow in 1983?

21. Cite a multi-volumed comparative history of North and South American literature. Which volume treats naturalism? Cite a multi-volumed history of Brazilian literature from 1500 through 1945.

22. With regard to dramatic structure, cite an example from a Shakespearean tragedy of an "exciting force."

23. Cite two bibliographies of Increase Mather. Give full bibliographical information, including number of entries and number of copies printed.

24. What is the conceptual first principle that French feminist theorist Monique Wittig seeks to dislodge? Give full publication information for her essay “One is Not Born a Woman.”

25. What journals are sponsored by Phi Beta Kappa, the National Council of Teachers of English, and the Southeastern Renaissance Conference?

26. What work of the modern author Syed Waliullah is best known outside India? What is it about? Where can one find reviews of Waliullah’s work? Into what European languages have his works been translated? When did he die?

27. In 1995-96 who published Georges Batailles’s *Blue of Noon* and *Literature and Evil*? What is the publisher’s New York address?

28. How many signed book reviews of Mary Renault’s historical novel *The Mask of Apollo* are listed in *Book Review Index* for 1966, the year of the novel’s publication? Has Peter Wolfe’s Twayne Series study of Mary Renault (1969) attracted much critical attention?

29. Cite three explicatory criticisms that appeared before 1990 of Dylan Thomas’s story “A Visit to Grandpa’s.” (Give full publication information.)

30. The second edition of Gita May’s *Diderot et Baudelaire, critiques d’art* was published in 1967. In what year does the *Bibliographic Index* first cite the second edition? Is the bibliography May includes primary, secondary, or both? How many pages long is it? Is it annotated?

31. Compile a list of renderings into modern English of *Sir Gawain and the Green Knight* published through 1900. Cite only rare editions, excluding post-1900 reprints. Which one of these is held by the Library of Congress?

32. Cite the author and title of a burlesque on Mary Wollstonecraft, published in Boston in 1795. Who else is satirized in this work?

33. Who is the author of a dissertation that is actually a critical edition of Lyly's *Mother Bombie*? Which text of the play is considered authoritative? Where in the dissertation is the play interpreted? What values are expressed through Lyly's use of antithetical structure?

34. Who printed the first (1616) edition of Chapman's translation of Homer? What was its original title? Which British libraries hold copies of the 1616 edition?

35. What was the Eleutheria? Name six classical writers who serve as a source for relevant information.

36. Note the sixteenth-century meanings of the adjective "tall" that differ from its twentieth-century meanings.

37. What is the "real value" of *Beowulf* as a historical authority, according to the editor of the 1881 edition? In what respect is *Beowulfiana* poor, according to Tolkien? Give full publishing information on Tolkein's essay.

38. Compile a list of Austrian authors born between 1920 and 1925.

39. Name a bibliography of books that were condemned in England between 1524 and 1683. When was it published? When and by what publisher was it reprinted? What other bibliography deals exclusively with British condemned books?

40. On what literary subject did Judith Ann Scheffler write a dissertation completed in 1978? To whom does Scheffler compare Herzog?

41. How many miles from Leicester was Bosworth Field? Where did Richard III's army take up its position? Some historians reject Richard's defeat at Bosworth as marking the end of the Wars of the Roses. What alternative date do they offer?

42. What was Ezra Pound's first book of poetry entitled? What famous poet wrote an early critical estimate of Pound for *Poetry*

magazine in 1916? Where were Robert Hillyer's articles on Pound and the Bollingen Prize Controversy published? What pamphlet contained a reply to Hillyer's stand? Name the book on Pound's trial written by his lawyer.

43. Complete Seanchan's speech in reply to these lines, as given in the New York 1904 and London 1904 printings of Yeats's *The King's Threshold.*

    500 Who could imagine you'd so take to heart
    501 Being driven from the council?

44. Identify: *The Morning Chronicle*, The Malone Society, the Oxford Movement.

45. Name the authors of four anthologies of Old English literature in modern English translation. Where can one find a modern English translation of the Old English poem "The Wife's Lament"? To what genre does "The Wife's Lament" belong? Where can one find an essay on the poem's narrative structure?

46. Cite an essay about *The New Yorker* magazine that was anthologized in 1970. How many other essays does the anthology contain? Who wrote "an appreciation" for the anthology?

47. What appears to be the primary nondramatic source for our knowledge of the celebrated British criminal Moll Cutpurse? Where else is she mentioned? What habit may have lengthened her life?

48. Who first used the term "overdetermination"? Who appropriated it for Marxist critical theory? In which fields has his work been influential?

49. How many printings of Ann Radcliffe's *Mysteries of Udolpho* were published in America through 1800?

50. Compile a list of new works by the historian Lacey Baldwin Smith that were published during the 1970s. (Exclude reprints but not new editions.) Where can Smith's *Elizabethan Epic* be seen?

51. When did Queen Elizabeth II succeed her father? What is her relationship to Queen Victoria?

52. Quote Blake's famous comment on *Paradise Lost*.

53. Cite explicatory criticisms by Stanley Edgar Hyman and Irving Howe of Flannery O'Connor's story "The Displaced Person."

54. In what periodicals did reviews of Philip Levine's *They Feed They Lion* first appear? What can you assume about the importance of this volume of poetry? Why?

55. List Arthur Arent's unpublished plays. What is the name of his television play? Cite two periodical sources dealing with his life and works.

56. Mention four collaborative works of photographers and writers funded by the Federal Writers Project during the Depression. Under the auspices of what umbrella agency did the FWP operate? How many people were involved in the Guidebook project?

57. Define "abo" and "goorie." Note their status, sources, variant forms, and earliest recorded uses.

58. Cite a critical work in print in 1995-96 dealing with gender issues affecting the legend of Dido. Name the press and provide its address.

59. Where can you find bibliographies of more than fifty entries, published between 1972 and 1976, dealing with Boris Pasternak? Note pages on which the bibliographies appear. Which bibliographies are annotated?

60. Who was the great organizer of the "new learning" of the English Renaissance? What was his most important work? What stylistic attributes does he recommend to a man of authority? Cite two works about him published in the 1960s.

61. What is H. C.'s 1579 ballad on Lord Darnley entitled? To what subject did C. W. address himself in 1624?

62. What countries and fields are treated in *Expressionism as an International Literary Phenomenon* edited by Ulrich Werner Weisstein? In which issue of *Comparative Literature Studies* is it reviewed?

63. Of the two words in each pair, which does Yeats use more frequently: day/night, young/old, man/woman? Cite the frequencies, and note whether you find any of the differences in frequency significant.

64. What was the program of the Connecticut Wits? What did the members of the Knickerbocker Group have in common? Who was the leader of the Bread and Cheese Club?

65. Cite a journal publishing English-language Marxist criticism. How many poems does it publish annually? How many reviewers read submissions?

66. Of the 1993 film reviews of *Ethan Frome* by Brown, Cramer, Kelleher, Lane, McCarthy, and Moss, which include the cast list? Which include pictures from the film?

67. What English-language works on Chaucer's "Miller's Tale" were published in 1975? (Explain abbreviations.)

68. Provide the title of a directory published in 1991, with entries for presses specializing in literary scholarship. To which Modern Language Association work is it a companion?

69. Who accused whom of plagiarism among the ancient Greeks?

70. How can the layperson immediately distinguish between the first printing and the second revised printing of Frank Norris's *McTeague*? Is there a discernible difference between the two printings of the revised edition? Name the bibliographer who examined these printings.

71. What are the tenets of these critical schools: Black Mountain, Geneva, Kailyard?

72. Using a specialized serial bibliography, note which romantic writers are discussed in Marlon B. Ross's 1989 book for Oxford University Press.

CHAPTER 6

ANNOTATED LIST OF SUPPLEMENTARY WORKS

DICTIONARIES, LITERARY ENCYCLOPEDIAS, HANDBOOKS, AND GUIDES

British and American Literature

S1. Bateson, F. W., and Harrison T. Meserole. *A Guide to English and American Literature.* 3rd ed. London: Longman, 1976.
A guide to authoritative editions, major criticism, reliable biographies, and literary background of principal British authors by two outstanding bibliographers. Meserole contributed a chapter on American writers born by 1900. Short critical essays and articles are for the most part excluded. Coverage generally extends through 1975. Arrangement is chronological by birthdate of the author. Special chapters are devoted to general works on English literature, literary criticism in English, and literary scholarship. Inter-chapters between bibliographies are historio-critical essays on the major literary periods. Index at back. Dated but still valuable. For supplemental works see Wright, below.

S2. Bracken, James K. *Reference Works in British and American Literature.* 2 vols. Englewood, CO: Libraries Unlimited, 1990.

Bracken is especially useful for full, evaluative descriptions of reference materials. Volume 1 provides annotated bibliographies of general sources, journals, research centers, and associations; volume 2 describes reference tools and journals (but not definitive editions) for some six hundred authors currently studied in literature courses—among them the 350 authors covered in Wright's 1970 *Reader's Guide to English and American Literature* (S8).

S3. Campbell, Oscar James, and Edward G. Quinn, eds. *The Reader's Encyclopedia of Shakespeare*. New York: Crowell, 1966.

Covers all facets of Shakespeare's life, theater, reputation, and works. Under entries for individual plays, probable sources and dates of composition, plot summaries, major criticisms, and production histories are provided. The appendices include a chronological outline of Shakespeare's life and works, transcripts of documents relating to Shakespeare, and a thirty-page classified bibliography. Alphabetically arranged; illustrated. A more recent, though less scholarly, compendium is Charles Boyce's *Shakespeare A-Z: An Essential Reference to His Plays, His Poems, His Life and Times, and More* (New York: Facts on File, 1990).

S4. Halkett, Samuel, and John Laing. *A Dictionary of Anonymous and Pseudonymous Literature*. New and enl. ed. by James Kennedy, W. A. Smith, and A. F. Johnson. 9 vols. [Vols. 8 (1900-1950) and 9 (Additions and Corrections) by Dennis E. Rhodes and Anna E. C. Simoni.] Edinburgh: Oliver and Boyd, 1926-62.

Halkett and Laing's work, which first appeared in 1882 and has been regularly updated, is still considered the best source for identifying the authors of anonymous and pseudonymous English literature. Arranged alphabetically by the first word of the title (other than articles), the dictionary notes the format and pagination of the first edition, the number of volumes, the place and date of publication, the name of its author, and the source for attribution of authorship. Coverage extends through 1949, and includes literary works in English printed abroad and literary works translated into English—but not periodical articles.

Volume 1 contains a list of authorities cited for attributions of authorship. The first supplement is found at the back of volume 6. Two indexes (the first to authors, the second to initials and pseudonyms) appear in volume 7. Volume 8 contains additions from 1900 through 1959, and volume 9 is composed of additions and corrections to all the earlier volumes. Both volumes 8 and 9 have their own indexes. A third chronologically arranged revised edition under the title *A Dictionary of Anonymous and Pseudonymous Publications in the English Language* is in progress (ed. John Horden (London: Longman, 1980-). Volume 1 covering 1475 through 1640 has appeared to date.

S5. Jones, Howard Mumford, and Richard M. Ludwig. *Guide to American Literature and Its Backgrounds Since 1890.* 4th ed., rev. and enl. Cambridge, MA: Harvard University Press, 1972.

A bibliographical outline including excellent headnote introductions to various aspects of the period covered. Jones and Ludwig present "in understandable order the combination of intellectual and sociological (political) event and literary productivity, which is at once the peril and the exhilaration of this enterprise" (General Introduction). Table of contents and publisher's abbreviations at front. Index of primary and secondary authors at back.

S6. Preminger, Alex, and T. V. F. Brogan, eds. *The New Princeton Encyclopedia of Poetry and Poetics.* 3rd ed. Princeton: Princeton University Press, 1993.

Signed, highly specialized articles on regional poetries, theory, prosody, genre, rhetoric, critical terms, etc., by such distinguished scholars as Jonathan Culler, Barbara Herrnstein Smith, Elaine Showalter, and O. B. Hardison. Articles range from brief to 20,000 words. Cultural studies are treated as well as literature. Ample quotation, bibliographies, and cross references. No entries for individual poets or poems. Also see T. V. F. Brogan's *New Princeton Handbook of Poetic Terms* (Princeton: Princeton UP, 1994).

S7. Temple, Ruth Z., and Martin Tucker, eds. *Twentieth-Century British Literature: A Reference Guide and Bibliography.* New York: Ungar, 1968.

Part I is an annotated reference guide to books about twentieth-century British literature. Noted in the table of contents are such categories as bibliographies of bibliographies, sources for biography, journals, histories, essays, and criticism subdivided by genre. Part II consists of bibliographies of some four hundred authors and is an expanded version of Temple and Tucker's *A Library of Literary Criticism: Modern British Literature*, 5 vols. (New York Ungar, 1966-85). Alphabetically arranged by author, Part II lists the author's works, their genres and publication dates, and reference sources about the author. A list of authors included is found on pp. 119-25. Index of authors at back. Note that another work is also entitled *Twentieth-Century British Literature*: the six-volume collection of critical essays and excerpts edited by Harold Bloom as part of the Chelsea House Library of Literary Criticism series (New York: Chelsea House, 1985-87).

S8. Wright, Andrew. *A Reader's Guide to English and American Literature.* Glenview, IL: Scott, Foresman, 1970.

A list of "the most reliable editions of the principal authors and the best works of biography and criticism" (Preface). Reference works on English, American, and foreign literatures are also included. Index of authors at back. A particularly useful work, although in need of updating. Supplement with Bracken (S2), Michael J. Marcuse, *A Reference Guide for English Studies* (Berkeley: U of California P, 1990), and with such evaluative annual surveys as those in *American Literary Scholarship* (S34), *The Year's Work in English Studies* (S42), and *Studies in English Literature: 1500-1900* (M19a).

S9. Wynne-Davies, Marion, ed. *The Bloomsbury Guide to English Literature: The New Authority on English Literature.* London: Bloomsbury, 1989. [Also published as *The Prentice Hall Guide to English Literature* (New York: Prentice, 1990).]

A more thoughtful version of the *OCEL* (M1), this work is notable for its fine background essays informed by history and theory as well as for its ready-reference section. Christopher Gillie's introductory essay, "Political History and Social Context," and John Drakakis's "Contemporary Approaches to Literature" set the tone for the periodized genre studies that follow. Arrow-shaped pointers before names and terms denote material in the reference section. A literary and a historical chronology in parallel columns appropriately conclude the volume.

Other Literature-Related Reference Works

S10. *Abstracts of English Studies: An Official Publication of the National Council of Teachers of English.* Calgary, Alberta: University of Calgary, 1958-91. [Originally published by the University of Colorado.]

This quarterly compilation of periodical abstracts, which ceased publication in 1992, was of particular importance to students of literature. Although restricted to English-language articles, its coverage was worldwide, and more than five hundred periodicals were screened. The resuscitation of *AES*, still useful as a retrospective source, would greatly benefit the field.

S11. Buttrick, George Arthur. *The Interpreter's Dictionary of the Bible.* 4 vols. New York: Abingdon, 1962. [Vol. 5, *Supplementary Volume*, 1976.]

Subtitled "an illustrated encyclopedia identifying and explaining all proper names and significant terms and subjects in the Holy Scriptures, including the Apocrypha with attention to archaeological discoveries and researches into the life and faith of ancient times." References are to the Revised Standard Version of the Bible. Signed articles by recognized scholars; bibliographies. Alphabetically arranged. Asterisks in the first four volumes indicate new material in the Supplement. This is a shorter updated version of the twelve-volume *Interpreter's Bible* (New York: Abingdon, 1951-57).

S12. Evans, Ivor H., ed. *Brewer's Dictionary of Phrase and Fable.* 14th ed. New York: Harper, 1989.

An updated nineteenth-century work described on the title page of earlier editions as "giving the derivation, source or origin of common phrases, allusions, and words that have a tale to tell." Phrases are colloquial or proverbial; allusions are historical, literary, mythological, biblical, etc. Alphabetically arranged. Both a reference tool and a browser's delight. A companion work is *Brewer's Dictionary of Twentieth-Century Phrase and Fable* (Boston: Houghton, 1992).

S13. Leach, Maria, and Jerome Fried, eds. *Funk and Wagnalls Standard Dictionary of Folklore, Mythology and Legend.* 2 vols.

1949-50; rpt. in 1 vol. with minor corrections. New York: Funk & Wagnall, 1972.

Representative but worldwide coverage of gods, heroes, nature lore and legends, folk dances and songs, festivals, rituals, children's games, magic, folklore scholars, etc. Some extensive signed scholarly articles with bibliographies. Greek mythology is de-emphasized. Alphabetically arranged.

S14. May, Herbert G., and Bruce M. Metzgar, eds. *The New Oxford Annotated Bible with the Apocrypha Revised Standard Version Containing the Second Edition of the New Testament and an Expanded Edition of the Apocrypha.* New York: Oxford University Press, 1977.

This ecumenical study Bible includes "Introductions, Comments, Cross-References, General Articles, Measures and Weights, Chronological Tables of Rulers, Maps, and Indexes." Annotations and articles by eminent biblical scholars. Particularly useful to students of literature are such articles as "Characteristics of Hebrew Poetry" and "Literary Forms in the Gospels." Table of Contents, p. v; indexes to annotations and maps at back.

S15. Oakman, Robert L. *Computer Methods for Literary Research.* Rev. ed. Athens: University of Georgia Press, 1984.

For the scholar with minimal computer experience, this book explains computer fundamentals, then describes specific literary applications such as concordance compilation, textual editing, and stylistic analysis. Extensive reference lists appear at the end of each chapter and in the Selected Bibliography, pp. 194-227. Diagrams, photographs, and index.

S16. Thompson, Stith. *Motif-Index of Folk Literature.* Rev. and enl. ed. 6 vols. Bloomington: Indiana University Press, 1955-58.

Subtitled "[a] classification of narrative elements in folktales, ballads, myths, fables, mediaeval romances, exempla, fabliaux, jest-books and local legends," the *Motif-Index* logically arranges these elements according to a numerical system and locates information about them by page references to standard folklore studies. To use this work fully and accurately, you must read the introduction.

S17. Wilson, F. P., ed. *The Oxford Dictionary of English Proverbs.* 3rd ed. Oxford: Clarendon, 1970.

Alphabetically arranged by significant words with cross-references. Earliest literary reference and some later references are cited. Also see *A Dictionary of American Proverbs* (New York: OUP, 1992), which contains some 15,000 proverbs currently used in Canada and the United States.

Language and Usage

S18. *The American Heritage Dictionary of the English Language.* 3rd ed. Boston: Houghton, 1992.

An excellent one-volume modern dictionary. Not only records the language but also suggests precise usage. Inclusion of slang and vulgar words. Readable entries: minimal use of abbreviation; no training in phonetics necessary for pronunciation. Profusely illustrated; many photographs. Essays on language and usage at front. Biographical and geographical entries at back.

S19. Gibaldi, Joseph. *MLA Handbook for Writers of Research Papers.* 4th ed. New York: MLA, 1995.

Although aimed at undergraduates, the *Handbook* provides sufficient information about the latest MLA documentation conventions to answer the needs of graduate students and those preparing journal articles for submission. Gibaldi expands the discussion of documentation practices in the *MLA Style Manual* (New York: MLA, 1985), adding an extensive treatment of electronic sources. Although MLA style is accepted by many scholarly journals, university presses, and graduate schools, some of these prefer Chicago style, described in *The Chicago Manual of Style: For Authors, Editors, and Copywriters*, 14th ed. (Chicago: U of Chicago P, 1993).

S20. Nicholson, Margaret. *A Dictionary of American-English Usage.* New York: Oxford University Press, 1957.

Based on the first edition of Fowler's *Modern English Usage*, Nicholson is still a useful guide to accurate diction. Presents correct idiomatic propositions, precise differences between similar words, preferred spellings, plurals, pronunciations, "vague" words to avoid, etc. Since Nicholson is out of print, look for it in the reference section of your library. Supplement with Wilson Follett's *Modern American Usage: A Guide*, ed. Jacques Barzun (New York: Hill and Wang, 1966); or the more recent, more liberal, and less prescriptive *Webster's Dictionary of English Usage* (Springfield, MA: Merriam-Webster, 1989).

S21. *Webster's New Dictionary of Synonyms*. Rev. ed. Springfield, MA: Merriam-Webster, 1984.

Subtitled "a dictionary of discriminated synonyms with antonyms and analogous and contrasted words," *Webster's* is both more comprehensive and simpler to use than Roget's classic *Thesaurus* (1852), the latter actually intended for a different purpose—discovering a specific word, having begun with a general concept. See Explanatory Notes (p. 32a) for analysis of entries. A particularly helpful feature of this dictionary is the citing of quotations from literature to discriminate synonyms through a context. A list of authors quoted, with dates and professional specialization, appears at the end.

Extraliterary Works

S22. *Steinberg's Dictionary of British History*. 2nd ed. Ed. S. H. Steinberg and I. H. Evans. London: Arnold, 1970.

Alphabetically arranged handbook of "political, constitutional, administrative, legal, ecclesiastical, and economic events" (Preface). Signed articles by a dozen specialists. No purely biographical entries.

S23. Walford, A. J. *Guide to Reference Material*. 6th rev. ed. London: Library Association, 1993.

This British publication is more comprehensive than Balay (M13), particularly in regard to British and European reference works. Evaluative annotations are often fuller.

Contents:

Vol. 1:	(1989) Science and Technology
Vol. 2:	(1990) Social and Historical Sciences, Philosophy and Religion
Vol. 3:	(1991) Generalia, Language and Literature, The Arts

Especially helpful are listings of reference materials on individual major writers. Each volume has its own two indices: of authors and titles, and of subjects. Volume 3 has a cumulative subject index.

S24. Wiener, Philip P., ed. *Dictionary of the History of Ideas: Studies of Selected Pivotal Ideas.* 5 vols. New York: Scribner's 1973-74.

Lengthy signed articles by internationally known scholars. The studies, necessarily selective, are of three kinds: "cross-cultural studies limited to a given century or period, studies that trace an idea from antiquity to later periods, and studies that explicate the meaning of a pervasive idea and its development in the minds of its leading proponents" (Preface). An extensive bibliography follows each article. Cross-references in brackets following the bibliography; the most significant references are printed in boldface. An Analytical Table of Contents for the four substantive volumes is found at the front of volume 1. A List of Articles, alphabetically arranged, and a List of Contributors with institutional affiliation and publications follow. Volume 5 is the index.

BIOGRAPHIES

British and American

S25. Bruccoli, Matthew J., ed. *Dictionary of Literary Biography.* Detroit: Gale, 1978-.

A critical and historical supplement to *Contemporary Authors* (M16) and the *Dictionary of American Biography* (S26) devoted primarily to substantial bio-critical essays on English-language writers, academics, and journalists. Chronologies and bibliographies are especially useful. Cumulative index to all preceding volumes in each new volume. *The Dictionary of Literary Biography* is also indexed in *Contemporary Authors.* Updating is achieved through the *Dictionary of Literary Biography Yearbook,* 1980- (currently through 1987). More recent *Yearbooks* survey publication, conferences, prizes, and include obituaries and interviews.

S26. Johnson, Allen, and Dumas Malone. *Dictionary of American Biography*. 22 vols. 1928-58; rpt. in 11 vols. New York: Scribner's 1958-64. (Continuing Supplements, 1973-.)

This American version of the British *Dictionary of National Biography* (M14) lists notable deceased Americans from all walks of life. Errata to the entire initial work are printed at the beginning of volume 1. Contributors are identified at the beginning of each volume. Arrangement is alphabetical, with bracketed bibliographies, including items never published, appended to each article. A *Comprehensive Index* (1990) contains six separate indexes to the original volumes and supplements through 1980: by subjects, contributors, birthplaces, schools and colleges, occupations, and topics. Volume 11 contains two supplements: the first updates through 1935, the second through 1940. Continuing Supplements under the auspices of the American Council of Learned Societies bring the *DAB* up to 1980 at this writing.

S27. *Who Was Who*. 3rd ed. London: Black; New York: St. Martin's, 1967.

Here are found the *Who's Who* entries for those no longer living. Vol. 1 contains the biographies of people who died during the period 1897-1915; vol. 2, 1916-1928; vol. 3, 1929-1940; vol. 4, 1941-50, etc. Further volumes appear at the close of each decade. Entries are alphabetically arranged within each volume. Use in conjunction with *Who Was Who: A Cumulated Index, 1897-1990* (New York: St. Martin's, 1991).

S28. *Who Was Who in America* [as of vol. 7]: *With World Notables. 8 vols. to date plus Historical Volume and Index Volume.* Chicago: Marquis, 1942-.

Volumes 1-4 are companion volumes to *Who's Who in America* (S29). Vol. 1 alphabetically lists the biographies of those who died during the period 1897-1942; vol. 2, 1943-1950; vol. 3, 1951-1960; vol. 4, 1961-1968; vol. 5, 1969-1973; vol. 6, 1974-1976. Continuing volumes bring this reference tool up through 1993 and include famous foreigners whose work influenced American history. The Historical Volume contains brief biographical sketches of notable Americans who died between 1607 and 1896 as well as biographical maps, historical charts, etc. The most recent index to all volumes appeared in 1993.

S29. *Who's Who in America.* Chicago: Marquis, 1899-.
This annual American work records information similar to that of its British counterpart (M15). Standards of admission are high. Some international notables are included. Works and dates are cited for authors, composers, etc. Index of retirees, index by region, and index by topic (professional and women) at the end of vol. 2 for each year. Note that *Who's Who in America* is a valuable tool for updating the *Dictionary of American Biography* (S26). Marquis also publishes index volumes to *Who's Who in America*, including a supplementary volume, *Who's Who in America: Geographic Index, Professional Area Index.*

World

S30. *Biography Index: A Cumulative Index to Biographical Material in Books and Mgazines* (1946-). New York: Wilson, 1947-. [With coverage back to January 1946.]
Quarterly issues with annual and triennial cumulations. Indexes books, periodicals, and obituaries, including those from *The New York Times.* Biography is interpreted broadly to include not only pure biography but also autobiography, letters, diaries, memoirs, journals, genealogies, bibliographies, and "creative" biographical works, i.e., plays, novels, etc. *Biography Index* is arranged in two parts: 1) by name of the biographee, and 2) by profession and occupation, authors being subdivided by nationality. On-line computer searching available.

S31. Magnusson, Magnus, ed. *Chambers Biographical Dictionary.* Cambridge: Cambridge University Press, 1990.
A one-volume international dictionary featuring readable articles and coverage from earliest times to the present. Contemporary figures are well represented. *Chambers* cites standard full-length biographies and notes an author's more important works. Pronunciation of difficult names is indicated. A supplement of the more recently famous and of necrology appears at front. The American edition, *Cambridge Biographical Dictionary*, the most recent edition of *Chambers*, includes more entries for those apt to be excluded from works of this sort.

BIBLIOGRAPHIES

Bibliographies of Bibliographies

S32. Howard-Hill, Trevor Howard. *Bibliography of British Literary Bibliographies*. 2nd ed. rev. and enl. Oxford: Clarendon, 1987. (Vol. 1 of a six-volume series with supplements entitled *Index to British Literary Bibliography*, 1969-; the remaining five volumes are still in first edition.)

British Literary Bibliography, 1970-79: A Bibliography, 1992. [Howard-Hill's first decennial supplement.]

Indexes bibliographies and textual notes published as books, as parts of books, or in periodicals, written in English and published in the English-speaking Commonwealth or the United States after 1890. Covers all of British literature, printing, and publishing from its beginnings. Detailed Table of Contents with categories for general, period, and regional bibliographies; for types of books, subjects, and literary authors. Shakespeare is excluded, being the subject of Vol. 2, *Shakespearean Bibliography and Textual Criticism* (1971). (Vol. 2 also includes material supplementary to Volume 1.) Index at back of contributing scholars, subjects (including literary authors), and a few titles of anonymous works, journals, and basic reference tools. Vols. 4 and 5—*British Bibliography and Textual Criticism: A Bibliography*, and *British Bibliography and Textual Criticism: A Bibliography (Authors)*—were published in 1979; Vol. 6, *British Literary Bibliography and Textual Criticism 1890-1969: An Index*, in 1980. Vol. 3 has not yet appeared.

S33. Nilon, Charles H. *Bibliography of Bibliographies in American Literature*. New York: Bowker, 1970.
Goes beyond Besterman (M17) and standard reference works on American literature, book publishing, and American history. Includes bibliographies, whether published separately or appearing as journal articles of parts of books. Divided into four main sections. Section

I—Bibliography—includes Basic American Bibliographies (arranged chronologically by historical period covered), Library of Congress and National Union Catalogs (arranged chronologically within topical areas), Other Basic Bibliographies, and General Bibliographies (these last two subsections and all following subsections arranged alphabetically by authors' names). Section II—Authors—is subdivided by centuries. Section III—Genre—includes Literary History and Criticism, Drama, Fiction, and Poetry. Section IV—Ancillary—is a miscellaneous category containing such entries as Cinema, Foreign Criticism of American Literature, The Negro, Themes and Types, etc. No cross-references. Author, title, and subject index at back. Patricia Pate Havlice's *Index to American Author Bibliographies* (Metuchen, NJ: Scarecrow, 1971) is useful as a supplement to Nilon for bibliographies published in periodicals.

Current Bibliographies: British and American

S34. *American Literary Scholarship: An Annual.* Durham, NC: Duke University Press, 1965-.

Annual, evaluative bibliographical essays by well-known scholars surveying significant contributions (books and dissertations as well as articles) to American literature. Begins with criticism written in 1963. Foreign contributors are listed as of 1975. Reviews of American literary theory studies are found under "Themes, Topics, Criticism." Table of Contents classifies authors, period, and genre. Key to abbreviations at front. Single index at back through 1974; separate author (secondary) and subject indexes thereafter. This is the counterpart for American literature of *The Year's Work in English Studies* (S42).

S35. *Annual Bibliography of English Language and Literature.* Modern Humanities Research Association. Leeds: W. S. Maney, 1921-.

A British publication, the "MHRA Bibliography" corresponds roughly to the *MLA International Bibliography* (M7), although the former is restricted to studies of English-language literatures and the English language itself. American critical works are listed, and there is particularly good coverage of literary newsletters and bibliographies of minor authors. Coverage of British studies is more extensive than the *MLAIB*'s. Listing of scholarly periodical reviews of secondary works on literature is a useful inclusion not found in the *MLAIB*. For these reasons *ABELL* should be regarded as a supplement rather than a replication of the *MLAIB*. Index, "Authors [both literary and critical] and Subjects Treated," at back of each volume. Two- to three-year time lag.

S36. Bryer, Jackson R., ed. *Sixteen Modern American Authors: A Survey of Research and Criticism*. New York: Norton, 1973.

—. *Sixteen Modern American Authors: A Survey of Research and Criticism Since 1972*. Durham, NC: Duke University Press, 1989.

This bibliography of twentieth-century writers is devoted to Sherwood Anderson, Cather, Hart Crane, Dreiser, Eliot, Faulkner, Fitzgerald, Frost, Hemingway, O'Neill, Pound, Robinson, Steinbeck, Stevens, William Carlos Williams, and Thomas Wolfe. The more recent volume has brief coverage through 1988.

S37. Gohdes, Clarence L., and Sanford E. Marovitz. *Bibliographical Guide to the Study of Literature of the U.S.A.* 5th ed. Durham, NC: Duke University Press, 1984.

An important selective, annotated bibliography, covering all genres and periods as well as many subjects related to American literature, e.g., Philosophy and Psychology in the United States, Religion, Arts Other Than Literature. Initial chapters are devoted to general reference tools and research techniques. Table of Contents and two indexes: Index of Subjects and Index of Authors, Editors, and Compilers. References are to numbered entries.

S38. Harbert, Earl N., and Robert A. Rees, eds. *Fifteen American Authors Before 1900: Bibliographical Essays on Research and Criticism*. Rev. ed. Madison: University of Wisconsin Press, 1984.

In this companion volume to *Eight American Authors* (S41), the editors treat Henry Adams, Bryant, Cooper, Crane, Dickinson, Edwards, Franklin, Holmes, Howells, Irving, Longfellow, Lowell, Norris, Taylor, and Whittier.

S39. Jones, Howard Mumford, and Richard M. Ludwig. *Guide to American Literature and Its Backgrounds Since 1890.* (See S5.)

S40. Leary, Lewis. *Articles on American Literature, 1900-1950.* Durham, NC: Duke University Press, 1954.

—. *Articles on American Literature, 1950-1967.* 1970

—. *Articles on American Literature, 1968-75.* 1979.

A selective but extensive listing of mostly English-language articles on American literature. Leary cumulates articles entered in *American Literature*'s quarterly checklists (M19,n.7), in the *MLA International Bibliography* and its antecedents (M7), and in a number of other sources (see his Introductions for bibliographical sources and periodicals examined). The Table of Contents must be used for all but author entries. Author listings and subject entries arranged alphabetically by critic. Unannotated. The 1968-75 supplement includes numerous additions and corrections to the preceding volumes. Another supplement is in progress.

Twentieth Century British Literature: A Reference Guide and Bibliography. (See S7.)

S41. Woodress, James, ed. *Eight American Authors: A Review of Research and Criticism.* Rev. ed. New York: Norton, 1971.
Based on the 1956 edition by Floyd Stovall, *Eight American Authors* is an excellent collection of bibliographical essays on all aspects of scholarship and criticism relating to Poe, Emerson, Hawthorne, Thoreau, Melville, Whitman, Twain, and James. Five of the original contributors have updated their essays; the other three are specialists in Melville, Whitman, and James, respectively. See *The Transcendentalists: A Review of Research and Criticism*, ed. Joel Meyerson (New York: MLA, 1984), for more recent research on this significant movement.

S42. *The Year's Work in English Studies* [1919-20]. Published for the English Association. London: Oxford University Press [later John Murray], 1921-.

An annual, selective critical survey consisting of extensive bibliographical essays; from these you can gain a sense of the current concerns of literary academicians. Coverage includes the best scholarly books and, less extensively, articles and notes by English and American critics on English and American literature and language, and the English-language literatures of Africa, Australia, India, New Zealand and the South Pacific, the Caribbean, and Canada. (Not every area is included in every volume.) From 1981 on, *YWES* has included a chapter on literary theory. Chapter subdivision is similar to that of the literary theory section of the *MLA International Bibliography* (M7). Note the subdivision on rhetorical theory. Table of contents for each volume. Indexes to secondary authors, literary authors, and subjects at back. *YWES* has a two- to three-year time lag.

World

S43. Baldensperger, Fernand, and Werner P. Friedrich. *Bibliography of Comparative Literature.* 1950; rpt. New York: Russell & Russell, 1960. (See S94.)

S44. *The British Library General Catalogue of Printed Books to 1975.* 360 vols. London: Bingley; New York: Saur, 1979-87. [Ongoing supplements.]

This is not a union catalog but rather a record of all printed books held by the national library of Britain from the fifteenth century. (Like the Library of Congress, the British Library has been awarded the copyright privilege.) It is essentially an author catalog; however, some title and subject entries are included, notably for biographies, which are entered under the name of biographee. Cross-references to anonyma, editors, translators, etc. are extensive. Subject indexes to the *General Catalogue* are available as are fiche cumulations.

S45. *Cumulative Book Index: A World List of Books in the English Language.* Minneapolis [later New York]: Wilson, 1898-.

As its subtitle indicates, *CBI* goes beyond a national bibliography in its scope, although *CBI* is most reliable with regard to books published in the United States. Currently excluding little more than government documents, maps, music scores, epehemera, and vanity publications, *CBI* catalogs a comprehensive listing of English-language books published since 1898. Since 1902 *CBI* has been arranged in a single alphabetical order of authors, subjects, and titles. Bibliographical information includes author or editor, translator, full title, series, volume number if a multivolumed work, edition, pagination, illustrator, binding (hardback or paper), price, and publisher. Standard Book Number (i.e., purchase number) and LC card number are cited when available. Author entries, located through cross-references, are most extensive. Publishers' addresses are listed at the back of each issue. *CBI* is currently published eleven times a year and cumulated annually. One of its chief virtues is its currency. Its permanent cumulations become supplements to the *United States Catalogue* (M24,n.2), thus forming the most comprehensive record of American book publishing from 1898 on.

S46. *Library of Congress Catalogs: Subject Catalog.* Washington, DC: Library of Congress, 1950-83.

Formerly *Library of Congress Catalog—Books: Subjects.* An alphabetically arranged listing by subject heading. For LC classifications, see *Library of Congress Subject Headings* (Washington: Library of Congress, 1910-). Note such broad headings as Fiction in English (which includes all individual works of fiction or collections of works of fiction written in English by a single author) or Fiction in English—Translations. Many subheadings and cross-references to related headings are employed; the same work may be entered under several headings. See the Guide to Use at the front of the first volume of each cumulation.

Almost all entries are located in at least one American library; the *NUC* supplies additional locations. Included are entries for books, pamphlets, periodicals, and other serials, in all languages, with imprint dates of 1945 or later, which have been catalogued from 1950 on. Entries are abbreviated versions of "LC Catalog" cards. This subject listing is issued quarterly with annual cumulations and some cumulations for longer intervals. Continued as *NUC: Books: LC Subject Index* (Washington, DC: Library of Congress, 1983-).

S47. *Year's Work in Modern Language Studies*, 1929/30-. Modern Humanities Research Association. Leeds: W. S. Maney, 1931-.

An annual evaluative bibliography of the most important work in Romance, Celtic, Germanic, and Slavonic languages and literatures. Author-subject index. Fairly current.

Retrospective Bibliographies

S48. Sabin, Joseph. *Bibliotheca Americana: A Dictionary of Books Relating to America, from its Discovery to the Present Time* [1892]. 29 vols. 1868-1936; rpt. Amsterdam: N. Israel, 1961; rpt. in one volume—Metuchen, NJ: Mini-Print, 1966. [After Sabin's death, the work was completed by Wilberforce Eames (vols. 14-20) and R. W. G. Vail (vols. 21-29).]

Sabin's bibliography differs most importantly from Evans's (M24) in that Sabin includes not only works published *in* the Western hemisphere but also books, periodicals, and pamphlets *about* the Americas, wherever these were printed and in whatever language. Sabin's coverage extends up to 1892; however, since "the Present Time" varied with the publication date of each volume, coverage is inconsistent. Arrangement is alphabetical by author, anonymous works being listed under the first word of the title other than an article. Full bibliographical information is given, often including the contents and location of reviews. Rare books are also located. The most extensive list of Library Location Symbols is found in volume 29, pp. 299-305. Despite restrictions in scope, discussed in the preface to the last volume, the *Bibliotheca Americana* is a monumental undertaking, ending appropriately with the words *Laus Deo*.

Also see John Edgar Molnar, *Author-Title Index to Joseph Sabin's Dictionary of Books Relating to America*, 3 vols. (Metuchen, NJ: Scarecrow, 1974); Lawrence S. Thompson, *The New Sabin: Books Described by Joseph Sabin and His Successors, Now Described Again on the Basis of Examination of Originals, and Fully Indexed by Title, Subject, Joint Authors, and Institutions and Agencies*, 10 vols. (Troy, NY: Whitston, 1974-86); and *European Americana: A Chronological Guide to Works Printed in Europe Relating to the Americas, 1493-1776*, ed. John Alden and Dennis Channing Landis (New Canaan: Readex, 1980—).

S49. Wing, Donald, comp. *Short-Title Catalogue of Books Printed in England, Scotland, Ireland, Wales, and British America and of English Books Printed in Other Countries 1641-1700*. 2nd ed. rev. and enl. Ed. John J. Morrison et al. New York: MLA, 1972-94.

Wing is a continuation of Pollard and Redgrave's *STC* (M23). Entries are numbered. Copies of works listed are located, though the compilers do not attempt a complete census. Periodical literature is excluded. For each citation, the editors supply the imprint, bibliographical information, references, and library or institutional locations. The works entered in Wing are available on microfilm. Note that Wing includes books printed in the American colonies through 1700. Wing is indexed in Paul G. Morrison, *Index of Printers, Publishers and Booksellers* [in Wing] (Charlottesville: U of Virginia P, 1958).

INDEXES AND DIRECTORIES

Indexes

S50. *Alternative Press Index: An Index to Alternative and Radical Publications* [1969-]. Baltimore: Alternative Press Center, 1970.

A subject index to creative and other writings "which amplify the cry for social change and social justice." See the headings Poems, Poetry (articles about poetry), Fiction/Samples of Writing (creative), Literature, Literary Criticism, Autobiographies, Bibliographies, Biography, Diaries/Memoirs, Directories, Indexes, Obituaries, Resources, and Speeches. Reviews of art, books, film, pamphlets, musicals, records, and theater are included. Beginning with volume 25 (1993), the fourth issue of each volume is an annual cumulation.

S51. *Arts and Humanities Citation Index*. Philadelphia: Institute for Scientific Information, 1977-.

A&HCI is useful for finding books, monographs, articles, and reviews related to your research subject and, if you have published, to find citations of your work. More than a thousand journals and some books are analyzed for citations. The *Index*, published semiannually, is accompanied by a *Guide* describing in detail *A&HCI*'s four-part format. If you know the author (X) of a work on your subject, you can look up X's name in the *Citation Index*. There you will find a listing of X's work cited in other writers' footnotes or bibliographies (or implied in their texts) and references to those citations. These secondary citations are likely to be relevant to your subject. The *Source Index* lists new work by X and cites all the secondary works to which X refers therein. The *Permuterm Subject Index* is a keyword-in-title index; the *Corporate Source Index* lists the organization with which X is affiliated. *A&HCI* is an on-line index.

Biography Index: A Cumulative Index to Biographical Material in Books and Magazines. (See S30.)

S52. *Book Review Digest*. New York: Wilson, 1905-.
Summarizes through quotation both favorable and unfavorable reviews of English-language fiction and non-fiction published or distributed in the United States and Canada. More than eighty popular and general (rather than specialized scholarly) periodicals are indexed. Length of reviews indicated. Arranged alphabetically by author of book reviewed. Subject and title index in each issue. Appears ten times a year with quarterly and annual cumulations. Use in conjunction with *Book Review Digest: Author/Title Index, 1905-1974*, 4 vols. (New York: Wilson, 1976); and *1975-1984* (1986).

S53. *British Humanities Index* [1962]. London: Bowker-Saur, 1963-.
(A continuation of *The Subject Index to Periodicals* [1915-61].)
A subject and author index to the humanities, "interpreted broadly to include the arts, economics, history, philosophy, politics, and society," drawn from some three hundred British periodicals. Creative writing and book reviews are excluded. Subheadings and lists of related headings for broad subjects. Appears quarterly with annual cumulations. The quarterly issues indexed by subject only; the annual cumulations provide two separate indexes: one by subject, the other by author. Within its field, *BHI* does for British periodicals what the *Essay and General Literature Index* (M27) does for American books. *BHI* can supplement the *MLA International Bibliography* (M7) and the *Annual*

Bibliography of English Language and Literature (S35) for articles from British periodicals.

Cumulative Book Index: A World List of Books in the English Language. (See S45.)

S54. Cushing, Helen, and Adah V. Morris. *Nineteenth Century Readers' Guide to Periodical Literature 1890-1899, with Supplementary Indexing 1900-1922.* 2 vols. New York: Wilson, 1944.
Indexes fifty-one mainly general and literary periodicals, seven of which are omitted from *Poole's* (S63). Supplementary indexing for some periodicals extends as far as 1922. Standard subject headings and cross-references. Author, subject, title, and illustrator index to articles, short stories, novels, plays, and poems. Note extensive entries under such broad headings as Drama—Criticisms and Poems. Also indexes book reviews but only under the author of the work reviewed. Many anonymous articles and reviews are identified from publishers' records. List of periodicals indexed at back.

S55. Goode, Stephen H., ed. *Index to American Little Magazines, 1900-1919: To Which Is Added a Selected List of British and Continental Titles for the Years 1900-1950, Together with Addenda and Corrigenda to Previous Indexes.* 3 vols. Troy, NY: Whitston, 1974. Supplements: 1920 through 1967.
An index of articles and reviews in American little magazines—avant garde literary journals devoted to aesthetic reform and experimentation—selected arbitrarily for their high literary value, degree of permanence, and omission from other indexes. Arranged by author of article and by subject in a single alphabet. The symbol + indicates the continuation of the article in subsequent issues. List of Abbreviations and Magazines Indexed at front of each volume.

S56. Goode, Stephen H., comp. *Index to Commonwealth Little Magazines* [1964-]. New York: Johnson Reprint [later Troy, NY: Whitston] 1966-.
Goode indexes commonwealth little magazines, using the same criteria for selection and the same arrangement found in the American index (S55). Current coverage from 1965 through 1992. Retrospective volumes in progress.

S57. *Humanities Index* [1974-]. New York: Wilson, 1975-. (Formerly *Reader's Guide to Periodical Literature Supplement* [1907-1915], *International Index to Periodicals* [1916-1964], *Social Sciences and Humanities Index* [1965-1974]).

Intended, in part, as a continuation of *Poole's Index* (S63). Currently an author and subject index to some 350 English and North American scholarly journals in the humanities. (Foreign journals were dropped in the 1940s.) Indexes original fiction, short stories, poetry, and drama. Author and subject entries are listed in a single alphabet. Each journal article is entered under its author and under a number of subject headings. Extensive subheadings, related headings, and cross-references. Full bibliographical information. An author listing of citations to book reviews at back. Quarterly with annual cumulations and permanent volumes cumulated for a longer period. *SSHI* is more up-to-date than the *MLA International Bibliography* (M7) or the *Annual Bibliography of English Language and Literature* (S35). Indexing most important literary journals, *SSHI* is to scholarly periodicals what the well-known *Readers' Guide to Periodical Literature* is to popular general interest magazines. On-line searching available.

S58. *Index to Little Magazines* (*Index to Literary Magazines*). Denver: Swallow, 1948-.

A continuation of *Index to American Little Magazines* (S55). Alphabetical author-subject listing. A gap in coverage between 1966 and 1985 may by filled by retrospective volumes to be published by the Coordinating Council of Literary Magazines: *The CCLM Index: An Annual Index to Literary Magazines*, comp. Stephen H. Goode (Greenwood, FL: Penkevill, 1986-).

Index Translationum: An International Bibliography of Translations (See S96.)

S59. *The Left Index: A Quarterly Index to Periodicals of the Left* [1984-]. Santa Cruz, CA: 1984-.

Indexes leftist journals but not newsletters or newspapers. Includes "anthropology, art, literature, economics, history, education, sociology, political science, philosophy, psychology, science, Black studies, [and women's studies]." This is a valuable source for book reviews; also valuable is the currency of coverage—within three to six months.

Chiefly an author index, *The Left Index* also contains a subject index, a book review index (arranged by author of the book being reviewed), a documents section (political speeches, statements, and resolutions), and a listing of recent leftist periodicals.

S60. *Literary Writings in America: A Bibliography.* 8 vols. Millwood, NY: KTO, 1977.

The goal of this vast WPA project was to list all creative American literature published in books and periodicals between 1850 and 1940. *Literary Writings* has a card format arranged alphabetically by author. Books reviews are entered both under the name of the reviewer, when known, and under the author of the work reviewed.

S61. *The New York Times Index, Prior Series* [1851-1912]. 15 vols. NY: Bowker, 1964-74.

The New York Times Index. Current Series. New York: New York Times, 1913-.

Personal Name Index to 'The New York Times Index' 1851-1974. 22 vols. Verdi, NV: Roxbury Data Interface, 1976-83. *1975-1989 Supplement.* 5 vols. 1990-91 (also corrects the original 22 volumes). From 1975 on *The Personal Name Index* is cumulated every five years, each cumulation starting with 1975.

For 1851 through August 31, 1858 in vol. 1 of the *Prior Series*, references are to issue numbers rather than to dates; that period is cumulated and arranged alphabetically by subject. Thereafter, the index is separated by year; references are to date, page, and column; "Supp" preceding a page number is a reference to that day's special supplement. Volume 2 has a table of contents indicating subdivisions. These are simplified in volumes 3-8 and discontinued in the remaining volumes.

The New York Times Index: Current Series [1913-] provides references to date, page, and column. Arrangement is alphabetical by subject, then chronological. Cross-references and brief abstracts of articles are included. For the student of literature, the *Personal Name Index*, covering 123 years in a single alphabet, greatly facilitates research on authors and critics mentioned in the *New York Times*. For productions of plays prior to 1871, look under "Plays—Reviews and

Notes"; thereafter, look under "Theatre—Reviews and Other Data on Specific Performances." References are to the year and page of the *Times Index* source volume. Roman numerals I-IV refer to the quarterly indexes (Jan.-March, Apr.-June, etc.) produced between 1913 and 1929. Also see *The New York Times Book Review Index 1896-1970*, 5 vols. (New York: Arno, 1973); and *The New York Times Obituaries Index 1858-1980* (New York: N.Y. Times, 1970-80).

S62. *Palmer's Index to the* [London] *Times Newspaper* [1790-1941]. London: Samuel Palmer, 1868-1943. Rpt. Nendeln, Liechtenstein: Kraus Reprint, 1956-66.

The Times Index. [1906-]. Reading: Research Publications, 1907-. Earlier volumes through 1960 rpt. Nendeln/ Liechtenstein: Kraus Reprint, 1968. Also entitled *The Annual Index . . . , The Official Index . . .*, and *Index to the Times.*

Palmer's subject index, dating back to 1790, covers 151 years. Beginning with the index for Oct.-Dec. 1867, it was published quarterly. Obituary notices, listed under "Deaths," are useful for contemporary biographical material. *The Times Index* now indexes not only *The Times* but also *The Sunday Times and Magazine*, *The Times Literary Supplement* (of special interest to literature students), *The Times Educational Supplement*, and *The Times Higher Education Supplement*. From 1977 on this subject index has been cumulated annually in two volumes. Book reviews are usually found under the author of the book reviewed, but sometimes under the rubric "Books," and then under the title.

S63. *Poole's Index to Periodical Literature*. 1802-81. Rev. ed., 1891. Supplements: 1882-1907. 6 vols. in 7, 1887-1908; rpt. Gloucester, MA: Peter Smith, 1963.

A subject or catchword (important word) index to some 590,000 articles, fictional works, and book reviews in 479 English and American periodicals. Coverage extends from 1802 to 1907. Creative literary works not lending themselves to a subject approach are entered under the first word of the title other than an article. Book reviews of such works are entered under the name of the author reviewed. Very brief articles and minor book reviews are omitted. A few British periodicals are not completely indexed. Bibliographical information lacks inclusive pagination and date. This last can be found most conveniently in Marian V. Bell and Jean C. Bacon, *Poole's Index: Date and Volume Key* (Chicago: Association of College and Research Libraries, 1957). C. Edward Wall, *Cumulative Author Index for Poole's . . . 1802-1906* (Ann Arbor: Pierian, 1971) is a computerized index arranged alphabetically by authors of articles cited in *Poole's*, noting volume, page, and column of articles and indicating single and multiple references. Also see Vinton A. Dearing, *Transfer Vectors for Poole's Index to Periodical Literature* (Los Angeles: Pison, 1967). *Poole's* has been in part superseded by the *Nineteenth Century Readers' Guide* (S54) and *The Wellesley Index* (S66), but only for some periodicals.

S64. Sader, Marion, ed. *Comprehensive Index to English-Language Little Magazines 1890-1970.* Series One. 8 vols. Millwood, NY: Kraus-Thomson, 1976.

Although not comprehensive, the *Index* analyzes one hundred magazines. Fifty-nine are American, devoted to poetry, fiction, and criticism. Organized alphabetically by author and subject. Signed book reviews are listed under the name of the reviewer. Cross-references identifying pseudonyms and variant forms of names. Genre or type of work cited for each listing; see Note to the User at the front of vol. 1. List of Magazines Indexed also at front of vol. 1.

S65. *Ulrich's International Periodicals Directory: A Classified Guide to Current Periodicals, Foreign and Domestic.* Providence, NJ: Bowker, 1932-.

Ulrich's is most helpful for those nonliterary subjects and creative writing serials that the *MLA Directory of Periodicals* (M30) does not cover. *Ulrich's* supplies brief entries for periodicals worldwide and on all subjects. Initially covering only periodicals published more than once a year, since 1988-89 *Ulrich's* has also included annuals and serials appearing at irregular intervals, e.g., yearbooks, transactions, proceedings, "advances in" and "progress in" publications. The extent of information provided varies. You may find full title and any former title, date of origin, publication frequency, subscription price, publisher's address, editor, special features (reviews, bibliographies, etc.), circulation, abstracting services, and more. Most descriptions, however, are brief, running about twenty-five words.

The first three volumes classify serials alphabetically by subject; subject terms are listed and cross-indexed at the beginning of volume 1. For literary periodicals the headings "Literary and Political Reviews," "Literature," and "Literature-Poetry" are most extensive. Other subject headings include such subgenres as science fiction, horror, and romance. Volume 4 lists serials available on CD-ROM and on-line, publications of international organizations, title changes, and cessations (periodicals discontinued since the previous edition of *Ulrich's*). The comprehensive title index at the end of volume 4 precedes ceased or suspended titles with a dagger. An upside-down solid triangle designates serials first published no earlier than 1991. The list of refereed serials in volume 4 is too incomplete to be useful. Volume 5 is devoted to American daily and weekly newspapers, and includes a list of newspaper cessations. In the future, *Ulrich's* plans to compile worldwide newspaper data. *Ulrich's Update* appears triannually. *Ulrich's Plus* is the CD-ROM quarterly version.

S66. *The Wellesley Index to Victorian Periodicals 1824-1900: Tables of Contents and Identification of Contributors with Bibliographies of Their Articles and Stories.* 5 vols. Toronto: University of Toronto Press; London: Routledge, 1966-89.

The Wellesley Index provides an accurate author index to forty-three major Victorian periodicals. Part A of each volume includes tables of contents (excluding poetry) for each issue of the periodicals covered. Most important, authors are identified with evidence for attribution of authorship and with bibliographies. This makes *The Wellesley Index* a significant attribution source, since Halkett and Laing (S4) exclude periodicals. Part B is the author index. Also included is an index of initials and pseudonyms.

HISTORIES AND ENCYCLOPEDIAS

S67. Edwards, Paul, ed. *The Encyclopedia of Philosophy.* 8 vols. New York: Macmillan; London: Collier, 1967. Supplement, 1996.

Signed scholarly articles on Eastern and Western philosophers, concepts, schools, movements, etc. Bibliographies; index at end of vol. 8.

S68. Eliade, Mircea. *The Encyclopedia of Religion.* 16 vols. New York: Macmillan, 1987. [1993 text edition.]

Signed articles, bibliographies, and a multidisciplinary approach. Coverage from the Paleolithic era to the present. The last volume contains the subject and name index, list of contributors, and an outline of contents.

S69. *Encyclopaedia Judaica.* 16 vols. New York: Macmillan, 1972. Decennial Books through 1992. Yearbook supplements.

This work supersedes the 1906 *Jewish Encyclopedia* but, like its predecessor, covers Jewish history, religion, literature, and customs from their beginnings to the present. Social, intellectual, geographic, and biographical information is included. Signed, scholarly, often exhaustive articles (the entry on Israel is equal in length to four good-sized novels), with appended bibliographies. Illustrations. Volume 1 is the index.

S70. *Encyclopedia of World Art.* 17 vols. New York: McGraw-Hill, 1959-87.

Comprehensive (includes architecture, sculpture, etc.). Scholarly signed monographs. Extensive bibliographies following major articles. Excellent plates comprising the second half of each volume. Vol. 15 is the index; vols. 16 and 17 are the supplements.

Leach, Maria and Jerome Fried. *Funk and Wagnalls Standard Dictionary of Folklore, Mythology and Legend.* (See S13.)

S71. Gray, Louis Herbert, et al. *The Mythology of All Races.* 13 vols. 1916-32; rpt. New York: Cooper Square, 1964.

Detailed, readable accounts of classical, Teutonic, Celtic, Slavic, Semitic, Asian, and other mythologies in separate volumes. Each volume has its own table of contents; a bibliography (now much in need of updating) and illustrations will be found at the end of each volume. Vol. 13 is the comprehensive index.

S72. Langer, William L., ed. *Encyclopedia of World History: Ancient, Medieval, and Modern.* 5th ed. Rev. and enl. Boston: Houghton, 1972.

Useful handbook, chronologically arranged. Maps, genealogical tables; appendix lists Roman emperors, popes, kings, colleges, etc. Detailed index.

S73. *New Catholic Encyclopedia.* 18 vols. New York: McGraw-Hill, 1967-89.

Subtitled "an international work of reference on the teachings, history, organization, and activities of the Catholic Church, and on all institutions, religions, philosophies, and scientific and cultural developments affecting the Catholic Church from its beginning to the present." Signed scholarly articles, many of them by non-Catholics, with appended bibliographies. Index in vol. 15. Vol. 16, Supplement, 1967-74; vol. 17: Supplement, Change in the Church; vol. 18: Supplement 1978-88. Unlike its predecessor, *The Catholic Encyclopedia* (1907-14), *The New Catholic Encyclopedia* is a religious encyclopedia in the broadest sense. The earlier work, however, is still well worth consulting.

S74. Sadie, Stanley, ed. *The New Grove Dictionary of Music and Musicians.* 20 vols. London: Macmillan, 1980.

Signed scholarly articles on all aspects of music (works, theaters, movements, instruments, theory, composers, performers, musicologists, etc.). Biographies and bibliographies. Unlike earlier editions, *The New Grove* (or Grove's sixth) gives full coverage to modern, popular, and ethnic music. Index of musical terms (non-western and folk) and index of contributors at back of vol. 20.

S75. Sills, David L., ed. *International Encyclopedia of the Social Sciences.* 19 vols. New York: Macmillan, 1968-91.

Signed scholarly articles on concepts, theories, and methods of Anthropology, Economics, Geography, History, Law, Political Science, Psychiatry, Psychology, Sociology, and Statistics. See articles on "literature" and "language." Biographies and bibliographies. Vol. 17 is the index, vol. 18, the Biographical Supplement, which includes bibliographies. Vol. 19, Social Sciences Quotations, includes an index and bibliographies.

Steinberg, S. H., and I. H. Evans, *Steinberg's Dictionary of British History.* (See S22.)

S76. Watson, George. *The Literary Critics: A Study of English Descriptive Criticism.* Enl. ed. London: Hogarth, 1986.
A history of criticism in England and, more recently, the United States by the editor of three volumes of the *New CBEL* (M5). Chapter 1. First Principles, in which Watson classifies types of criticism and discusses the nature of descriptive criticism, is of value to all students of literature regardless of their particular interests. Chapter bibliographies precede the index. A highly readable work.

Wiener, Philip P. *Dictionary of the History of Ideas.* (See S24.)

CHILDREN'S LITERATURE

Abstracts

S77. *Children's Literature Abstracts.* Birmingham, England: International Federation of Library Associations and Institutions, 1973-.
Publishes English-language abstracts of children's literature articles by scholars of all nationalities. Twice a year quarterly supplements abstract books and pamphlets.

Handbooks, Bibliographies, and Indexes

S78. Bingham, Jane, and Grayce Scholt. *Fifteen Centuries of Children's Literature: An Annotated Chronology of British and American Works in Historical Context.* Westport, CT: Greenwood, 1980.
Chronological annotated entries from A.D.523 through 1945 of books used by and/or written for children. Historical material relevant to children's literature precedes each period division (Anglo-Saxon, Middle English, Renaissance, etc.). Bibliographies of secondary sources, chronologies of British and American children's periodicals, key to pertinent book collections, list of facsimile editions and publishers, author-illustrator-printer index, and a title index.

S79. Carpenter, Humphrey, and Mari Prichard. *The Oxford Companion to Children's Literature*. Oxford: Oxford University Press, 1984.
Entries range from legends and medieval romances (e.g., *Sir Bevis of Hampton*) to current writings, magazines, and media characters. Illustrator and printer entries. American, English, and some foreign works are represented. Publishing history and evaluation of present status for major works. Entries on the history of children's literature in all countries for which information was accessible.

S80. *Children's Books in Print: An Author, Title, and Illustrator Index to Children's Books*. NY: Bowker, 1969-.
An annual variant of *Books in Print* (M29). Excludes textbooks, toy books, and workbooks. Like *BIP*, *CBIP* is accompanied by a *Subject Guide*.

S81. *Children's Literature Association Quarterly*, "Bibliography."
Volume 8 (1983) of *ChLAQ* features an annotated bibliography reinstated in 1989 as a regular serial bibliography. Coverage is international and includes the widest possible range of subjects. For updating retrospective bibliographies, also see the Subject Index to the *MLA International Bibliography* (M7) under the heading "Children—as Audience"; and its British counterpart, the *Annual Bibliography of English Language and Literature* (S35).

S82. Haviland, Virginia, and William Jay Smith, comps. *Children and Poetry: A Selective, Annotated Bibliography*. 2nd rev. ed. Washington, DC: Library of Congress, 1979.
The bibliography is divided into five sections: Rhymes (Mother Goose and other traditional rhymes are omitted for lack of space), Poetry of the Past, Twentieth-Century Poetry, Anthologies, and World Poetry. Ample primary and secondary quotations. Index of authors, illustrators, and anthology titles.

S83. Haviland, Virginia, et al. *Children's Literature: A Guide to Reference Sources*. Washington, DC: Library of Congress, 1966. Supplements, 1972, 1982.
An extensive annotated subject bibliography of "Books, articles, and pamphlets selected on the basis of their estimated usefulness to adults concerned with the creation, reading, or study of children's books"

(Preface). Subject headings include History and Criticism, Authorship, Illustration, Bibliography, and National Studies (Eastern and Western Europe, Latin America, Asia, and South Africa). New subjects are introduced in the Supplements, which also update sources for subjects in the earlier volumes. At back, a directory of associations and agencies under whose auspices various entries were published; also an author-title-subject index.

S84. Hendrickson, Linnea. *Children's Literature: A Guide to the Criticism*. Reference Publications in Literature. Boston: G. K. Hall, 1987.

Currently the best annotated bibliography of criticism in English of children's literature in all languages. Broadly based—significant articles, books, and dissertations from disparate disciplines and diverse publications, popular as well as scholarly. Favors twentieth-century works. A separate index to critics, another to authors, subjects, and titles.

S85. Leif, Irving P. *Children's Literature: A Historical and Contemporary Bibliography*. Troy, NY: Whitston, 1977.

Leif claims to list "virtually all the literature about children's literature" (Preface), including theses, dissertations, and some non-English-language works. He cites works on contemporary trends, historical background, schoolbooks, religious tracts, individual authors, illustrators, and the children's book industry. His scope is international.

S86. Nakamura, Joyce, ed. *Children's Authors and Illustrators: An Index to Biographical Dictionaries*. 5th ed. Gale Biographical Index Series, no. 2. Detroit: Gale, 1995.

A monumental feat of indexing. Some writers for adults (Twain, Steinbeck) included. Excludes periodicals other than *Biography Index* (S30). Key to source abbreviations ["Publication Codes"] at front.

Criticism

S87. Bator, Robert. *Signposts to Criticism of Children's Literature*. Chicago: American Library Association, 1983.

A valuable collection of critical essays by such distinguished scholars and writers as Francelia Butler, Lois Kuznets, Isaac Bashevis Singer, and Clifton Fadiman, who discuss the definition, status, and territories of children's literature.

S88. Chevalier, Tracy, ed. *Twentieth-Century Children's Writers.* 3rd ed. Chicago: St. James, 1989.

Alphabetically arranged bio-bibliographical listings with signed critical essays and some authorial comment. Includes citations for works illustrated by the authors. Appendices: nineteenth-century writers; foreign-language writers whose works have been translated into English.

S89. *Children's Literature Research: International Resources and Exchange.* München: Saur, 1991.

Useful essays from the First International Conference (1988) surveying current international research, including criticism. A bibliography is appended.

S90. *Children's Literature Review: Excerpts from Reviews, Criticism, and Commentary on Books for Children and Young People.* Detroit: Gale, 1976-.

This annual series currently includes several hundred authors. Format is similar to *Contemporary Authors* (M16) and its spin-offs: *Contemporary Literary Criticism* and *Twentieth Century Literary Criticism*, etc. These are cross-referenced in the cumulative author index. Also includes cumulative index to nationalities and titles. For locating current reviews, use *Children's Book Review Index* (Detroit: Gale, 1975-); Master Cumulation 1969-81, 4 vols. (1982).

Journals

S91. *Children's Literature Association Quarterly.* Winnipeg, Canada: The Association, 1974-.

ChLAQ, the organ of the Children's Literature Association, is concerned with the history and criticism of children's literature. Issues are often devoted to special topics. Articles, book reviews (usually one per issue), paper calls, conference announcements, and the children's literature bibliography (see S81, above).

S92. *Children's Literature in Education: An International Quarterly.* New York: Human Sciences, 1970-.

Primarily covers the United States, Canada, and the United Kingdom. Despite the title, articles and essay reviews are currently more critical than pedagogical.

S93. *The Lion and the Unicorn: A Critical Journal of Children's Literature.* Baltimore: Johns Hopkins, 1977-.

International coverage of children's literature. Articles, reviews, and interviews. Issues are devoted to particular genres or themes.

COMPARATIVE AND WORLD LITERATURE

Bibliographies

S94. Baldensperger, Fernand, and Werner P. Friedrich. *Bibliography of Comparative Literature.* 1950; rpt. New York: Russell & Russell, 1960. [The reprint adds a bibliography on Scandinavia.]

A monumental listing arranged in four parts. Book I deals with the theory of comparative literature; with intermediaries between one literature and another; and with common themes, subjects, and genres. Book II covers the Orient and Antiquity, both generally and with respect to individual authors. Book III, Aspects of Western Culture, traces broad literary and social influences from the end of the classical period to modern times. Book IV lists specific studies of the period. The detailed Table of Contents substitutes for an index. Annual bibliographies in *The Yearbook of Comparative and General Literature* (S98) supplement this older work through 1969. For more recent studies see the *MLA International Bibliography* (M7).

S95. *The British Library General Catalogue of Printed Books to 1975.* (See S44.)

Cumulative Book Index (See S45.)

S96. *Index Translationum: An International Bibliography of Translations.* Paris: International Institute of Intellectual Cooperation [later UNESCO], 1932-40, 1948-89.

An annual listing of translated books published in seventy-five countries. Arranged alphabetically by French names of countries, then under one of ten broad category headings found on page 9 of *IT, 1970.* References include author, title, translator, place of publication, date (if other than the year of listing), pagination, special features, and price. The language in which the original work was written and its original title are noted in italics. Table of Contents at front; index of original authors and anonymous works at back with references to numbered entries. Translations published in countries in which English is either the primary or one of the primary languages have been cumulated for the years 1948-68 in *Cumulative Index to English Translations 1948-1968*, 2 vols. (Boston: Hall, 1973).

Library of Congress Catalogs: Subject Catalog. (See S46.)

S97. *The Literatures of the World in English Translation: A Bibliography.* 3 vols. New York: Ungar, 1967-70.

This work consists of *The Greek and Latin Literatures*, ed. George B. Parks and Ruth Z. Temple (1968); *The Slavic Literatures*, comp. Richard C. Lewanski (1967); and *The Romance Literatures*, ed. George B. Parks and Ruth Z. Temple, 2 parts (1970). These volumes can serve as a *guide* to non-English literatures in that the background sections on general literature, on particular national literatures, and on literary periods are as valuable as the author listings. Moreover, in volumes 1 and 3 literature is interpreted in its widest sense as writings in the humanities. The most important translations are indicated by an asterisk.

Thompson, Stith. *Motif-Index of Folk Literature.* (See S16.)

S98. *Yearbook of Comparative and General Literature.* University of North Carolina [later Bloomington: University of Indiana], 1952-.

An annual journal devoted primarily to literary and interdisciplinary articles but that includes 1) a "Bibliography on the Relations of Literature and the Other Arts"; 2) listings of new translations into English, collected for 1960 through 1980, and intended as a supplement to the *Bibliography of Comparative Literature* (S94); and 3) the annual bibliography of comparative literature for 1949-69 in the volumes for 1952-70, collected in *Bibliography of Comparative Literature 1950-1970, Cumulative Indexes.*

Year's Work in Modern Language Studies (See S47.)

Dictionaries, Encyclopedias, and Guides

S99. Avery, Catherine A., ed. *The New Century Classical Handbook.* New York: Appleton, 1962.

Unlike *The Oxford Classical Dictionary* (M11), this handbook is aimed at the general reader; bibliographies and exact reference citations are omitted, but plot summaries, a pronunciation guide, drawings, photographs, and maps are included. Coverage extends only through A.D.68.

S100. Banham, Martin, ed. *Cambridge Guide to World Theatre.* Cambridge: Cambridge University Press, 1988.

A corrective to works primarily concerned with western drama, Banham emphasizes drama in the rest of the world. "World Theatre" is used inclusively, comprehending folk as well as professional performances. Television, radio, opera, ballet, and the various individuals responsible for production are also treated. Some bibliography.

S101. Benét, William Rose. *The Reader's Encyclopedia.* 3rd ed. New York: Harper and Row, 1987.

Contents and treatment similar to the *OCEL* (M1), but covers all literatures. Alphabetically arranged. Cross-references in small capitals.

S102. Benson, Eugene, and L. W. Conolly. *Encyclopedia of Post-Colonial Literatures in English.* 2 vols. London: Routledge, 1994.

Specialists (nearly six hundred of them) write on the literatures of "such diverse countries as Canada, Nigeria, Sri Lanka, and New Zealand" (Introduction, xxv). Excluded are the literatures of the British Isles, albeit these regions, whether as victims or victimizers, also participated in the colonial experience. Major subjects are subdivided, e.g., "Australian Literature" includes the subdivisions "Ireland and Irish

Values in Australia," and "Jewish Writing in Australia." Bolding indicates cross-references. Further reading lists are provided for some entries. The table of contents lists main authors and topics. Exceptionally full author-title, subject index at back of volume 2.

S103. Blamires, Harry, ed. *A Guide to Twentieth Century Literature in English.* London: Methuen, 1983.

This handbook, with author entries only, covers the United Kingdom, Ireland, Canada, the Caribbean, Australia, New Zealand, and a number of African and Asian countries but not the United States. So broad a scope encourages us to understand English literature globally as well as nationally.

S104. Buchanan-Brown, J., ed. *Cassell's Encyclopaedia of World Literature.* [2nd. ed.] Rev. and enl. 3 vols. London: Cassell, 1973.

Signed articles, some of substantial length; bibliographies are appended to all biographies and to many other entries. Volume 1 contains histories of individual literatures, literary terms, genres, schools, movements, themes, and topics (including influential literary works). Volumes 2 and 3 are devoted to author biographies (with selected primary and secondary bibliographies) and to anonymous works; author and title entries arranged in a single alphabet. Credentials of contributors at front of Volume 1. Contributors's initials, Key to Special Signs, and Notes for the User at front of each volume.

S105. Gassner, John, and Edward Quinn, eds. *The Reader's Encyclopedia Encyclopedia of World Drama.* New York: Crowell, 1969.

Unlike Phyllis Hartnoll's *Oxford Companion to the Theatre* (S106), which emphasizes popular drama and production aspects, *The Reader's Encyclopedia of World Drama* is concerned with drama as literature. There are no entries for actors, acting companies, theaters, and the like. A valuable inclusion is the appended Basic Documents in Dramatic Theory. Alphabetically arranged; illustrated.

S106. Hartnoll, Phyllis, ed. *The Oxford Companion to the Theatre.* 4th ed. Oxford OUP, 1983.

Hartnoll takes all drama for her province, from its earliest forms to the present. Emphasis is upon plays in performance. Motion pictures are excluded. Appended are a lengthy classified bibliography of theater books and a wealth of annotated illustrations.

S107. Kienzle, Siegfried. *Modern World Theater: A Guide to Productions in Europe and the United States since 1945.* Trans. Alexander and Elizabeth Henderson. New York: Ungar, 1970.

This reference work on post-World War II drama provides extensive plot summaries. Arranged alphabetically by author. Includes data on translations. Index to play titles at end.

S108. Klein, Leonard S. *Encyclopedia of World Literature in the 20th Century: A Guide.* 5 vols. New York: Ungar 1981-93 [Vol. 5, Supplement and Index, ed. Steven R. Serafin.]

Similar to the Penguin Companion series (M12), though entries are longer and limited to the twentieth century. Excellent discussion of literary subjects as well as authors. Signed articles of a biographical and critical nature. Primary and secondary bibliographies. Literatures of Africa and the Far East in all volumes. Volume 5, the 1993 supplement, draws on the literature and criticism of the 1980s for additions and reevaluations. Alphabetically arranged; plates; cumulative index to all volumes at back of volume 5.

S109. Matlaw, Myron. *Modern World Drama: An Encyclopedia.* New York: Dutton, 1972.

Articles on dramatists and dramas. For playwrights Matlaw provides biographies and bibliographies (primary and secondary), for plays articles discussing publication and original production. Plot summaries. Some articles treat the drama of various countries; others deal with movements, schools, etc. Emphasis on American and European drama. Illustrated. Index of characters as well as a general index of authors, titles, geographic areas, and dramatic terms.

S110. Orr, Leonard. *A Dictionary of Critical Theory.* 2nd ed. U of Chicago, 1995.

Ranging from the earliest times to the present, Orr defines and contextualizes Chinese, French, German, Greek, Japanese, Latin, Russian, Sanskrit, and English terms. Cross-references and capsule bibliographies. Extended bibliography, pp. 447-63.

S111. Pynsent, Robert B. *Reader's Encyclopedia of Eastern European Literature.* New York: HarperCollins, 1993. [In the UK entitled *Everyman Companion to East European Literature.*]

Entries for writers, movements, etc. from the former Russian, Turkish, Prussian, and Austrian empires, an area circumscribed by Finland, Greece, Albania, Georgia, Armenia, and Czechoslovakia. Writers are located within their cultural histories. Biographies are complemented by analyses of work; three translations are listed for each writer. Two sections follow the A through Z entries: one on anonymous, collective, and oral tradition texts; another containing brief histories of individual literatures, alphabetically arranged according to language. For explanation of the bibliographic references, see Abbreviations at the front of the volume. Three indexes: authors, anonymous works, and general.

S112. Seymour-Smith, Martin. *Macmillan Guide to Modern World Literature.* 3rd ed. London: Macmillan Reference Books, 1985.

One man's survey of this enormous area. Far more readable, provocative, and sometimes infuriating than standard compendiums. Abbreviations at front refer to convenient translations. Text is arranged alphabetically by country or area of the world, about which Seymour-Smith initially generalizes. For individual authors, see the index at back, which is preceded by brief bibliographies of reference works and criticism ordered by area.

S113. Shipley, Joseph T., ed. *Dictionary of World Literary Terms: Forms, Technique, Criticism.* Rev. and enl. Boston: The Writer, 1970.

Entries for literary terms are not confined to Europe and the Americas, as are the historical surveys of literary criticism in Part II. Signed articles by authorities; bibliographies. Included in Part III is a selected list of critics and works devoted to countries not covered in the critical surveys. Part III is arranged chronologically under the national heading.

S114. Ward, Philip, ed. *Oxford Companion to Spanish Literature.* New York: Oxford University Press, 1978.

The *OCSL* is not limited to writings of Spanish authors in Spanish but includes entries for authors and works from Central and South America and the Philippines as well as works in Basque, Catalan, and Galician. Covering the vast period from Roman Spain to 1977, Ward nevertheless includes "many young writers. It is probably true to say that of all Latin American writers, the majority are alive and writing today" (Preface). Historical and political references are scanted in favor of extensive bibliographies. List of abbreviations used precede the "A" entries.

Journals

S115. *Comparative Literature.* Eugene: University of Oregon Press, 1949-. Quarterly.

S116. *Comparative Literature Studies.* University Park: Pennsylvania State University [formerly Urbana: University of Illinois Press], 1963-. Quarterly.

FILM

Bibliographies and Filmographies

S117. *The American Film Institute Catalog of Motion Pictures Produced in the United States.* New York: Bowker, 1971-. [To date, 1911-1940 and 1961-70; also see the 1893-1910 volume (Scarecrow, 1995).]

The American Film Institute hopes to catalog all films made in the United States, whether or not they are extant. Commercial and production information is followed by cast credits, a genre designation, plot summary, and a list of terms under which the film is indexed in the subject index. A major primary source.

Journal of Modern Literature. (See M19f).

MLA International Bibliography. (See M7,n.3.)

S118. Rehrauer, George. *The Macmillan Film Bibliography.* 2 vols. New York: Macmillan, 1982.

Evaluative descriptions of more than 670 nonfiction books about films. Volume 2 is a three-part index: by subject, author, and script. References are to numbered book entries in volume 1. Since Rehrauer lists only books, his work can be supplemented by Frank Manchel, *Film Study: An Analytical Bibliography.* 4 vols. Rutherford, NJ: Fairleigh Dickinson UP; London: Associated UP, 1990, an annotated subject guide to films and works about film in English.

Dictionaries, Handbooks, and Guides

S119. Armour, Robert A. *Film: A Reference Guide.* Westport, CT: Greenwood, 1980.

A bibliographic essay describing and evaluating important English-language books on film, especially popular American films. Film history, production, criticism, and genre are among the subjects treated. Chapter 11 is devoted to reference works and periodicals. An enumerative bibliography follows each chapter. Subject and author-editor-interviewee indexes at back.

S120. Beaver, Frank Eugene. *Dictionary of Film Terms: The Aesthetic Companion to Film Analysis.* Rev. ed. New York: Twayne; Toronto; Maxwell Macmillan Canada; New York: Maxwell Macmillan International, 1994.

Focuses on terms associated with the construction of films rather than on their subject matter. Chronology of film history at back. An index to terms, another to titles.

S121. Dimmitt, Richard Bernard. *A Title Guide to the Talkies: A Comprehensive Listing of 16,000 Feature-Length Films from October, 1927, until December, 1963.* 2 vols., New York: Scarecrow, 1965. [Continued by Andrew A. Aros with new subtitles, *1964 through 1974* (1977) and *1975 through 1984* (1986).

Dimmitt locates and annotates the sources of major American films, primarily in other genres (short fiction, drama, poetry). Aros includes foreign films that were shown in the United States. Arranged by title with an author index.

S122. Fisher, Kim N. *On the Screen: A Film, Television, and Video Research Guide.* Reference Sources in the Humanities Series. Littleton, CO: Libraries Unlimited, 1986.

An evaluative guide to post-1950s film and television productions in the United States. Categories are based on various types of reference works. Two indexes, the first to authors and titles, the second to subjects.

S123. Katz, Ephraim. *The Film Encyclopedia.* 2nd ed. New York: HarperCollins, 1994.

A one-volume alphabetically arranged encyclopedia covering world cinema. Particularly useful for biographies of directors, actors, and production artists. Filmographies accompany many entries. Film terms, organizations, etc. also included.

S124. Magill, Frank N. *Magill's Survey of Cinema: English Language Films.* Englewood Cliffs, NJ: Salem, 1980-81. First Series, 4 vols. Second Series, 6 vols.

Articles of several pages on films going back to 1972. An account of the story is interwoven with discussion of the direction, characterization, screen writing, and cinematography. Each entry includes date of release, running time, and credits. Brief glossary at front of volume 1 of Series 1. Series alphabetically arranged by title. Cumulative index in last volume of each series. Update with *Magill's Cinema Annual* (1982-), surveying the films of the previous year. Included are retrospective films, obituaries, awards, and indexes by title director, screenwriter, cinematographer, editor, art director, music director, performer, and subject. Also see *Magill's Survey of Cinema: Silent Films*, 3 vols. (1982); and *Magill's Survey of Cinema: Foreign Language Films*, 8 vols. (1985).

S125. Thomas, Nicholas, ed. *The International Dictionary of Films and Filmmakers.* 2nd ed. 5 vols. Chicago: St. James, 1990-1994.

Volume 1, Films; Volume 2, Directors/Filmmakers; Volume 3, Actors and Actresses; Volume 4, Writers and Production Artists; Volume 5,

Title Index. Despite its title, this work is limited to North American and Western European works. Aside from descriptive and evaluative entries, the *Dictionary* provides highly useful bibliographies. For films, the editor lists scripts, books, articles, and reviews; for film personnel, a filmography and works by and about them.

Indexes and Digests

S126. *Essay and General Literature Index.* (See M27.)

S127. *International Index to Film Periodicals: An Annotated Guide.* London: International Federation of Film Archives, 1973-.
This important annual subject guide is divided into three parts: general subjects (e.g., adaptations, aesthetics, censorship); individual films; and biography. Annotations indicate the type of item—article, interview, review—and briefly describe the content. Director and author indexes at back.

S128. *New York Times Film Reviews 1913-.* New York: *New York Times*, 1913/68-. [New volumes every second year.]
Chronologically arranged reproductions of *New York Times* reviews. Index of titles, film companies, performers, and other personnel. Includes awards and photographs. Reviews for 1913-1968 published in six volumes. Current supplements contain reviews for 1991-92.

LITERARY THEORY

Bibliographies

S129. Marshall, Donald G. *Contemporary Critical Theory: A Selective Bibliography.* New York: MLA, 1993.
Marshall introduces an extensive number of theories by such thinkers as Bakhtin, Barthes, Benjamin, Kristeva, and Lacan. Author summaries

and annotated bibliographies of works in English. Useful cross-references and an author/translator index.

S130. Orr, Leonard, comp. *Research in Critical Theory since 1965: A Classified Bibliography*. Bibliographies and Indexes in World Literature 21. New York: Greenwood, 1989.
An unannotated bibliography of modern theoretical works, including American dissertations. French and German books and articles are also included. Coverage through 1987 with some entries for 1988. Indexes to subjects and major theorists; to twelve theoretical categories (structuralism, semiotics, Marxism, etc.); and to authors. Also see Orr's *Dictionary of Critical Theory* (S110).

For ongoing bibliographies, see the following:

American Literary Scholarship: An Annual. (See S34.)
Reviews of American literary theory studies under "Themes, Topics, Criticism."

MLA International Bibliography. (See M7.)
This is the most extensive source for theory; unfortunately, it is unannotated. Use the Classified Listings, volume 4: General Literature and Related Topics. The heading Literary Theory is subdivided into deconstructionist, feminist, formalist, hermeneutic, linguistic, Marxist, narrative, phenomenological, philosophical, postmodernist, poststructuralist, psychoanalytic, psychological, reader-response, reception, rhetorical, semiotic, sociological, and structuralist.

The Year's Work in English Studies. (See S42).
From 1981 on, *YWES* has included a chapter on literary theory. Here you will find extensive evaluative bibliographic essays on important books and articles of the year preceding publication of the annual volume. (*YWES* has a two- to three-year time lag.) Chapter subdivision is similar to that of the *MLAIB*'s literary theory section (above). Two indexes at back: to critics and to authors and subjects treated.

Introductory Surveys and Anthologies

S131. Eagleton, Terry. *Literary Theory: An Introduction.* Minneapolis: University of Minnesota Press, 1983.

Now a classic, this is a witty and lucid overview of current theoretical schools. Eagleton considers the origins of present-day movements in linguistics, philosophy, and realpolitik. Written from a Marxist perspective. Bibliography: pp. 223-31.

S132. Greenblatt, Stephen and Giles Gunn, eds. *Redrawing the Boundaries: The Transformation of English and American Literary Studies.* New York: MLA, 1992.

An anthology of essays by major scholars discussing their respective specialties in light of the new approaches generated by contemporary theory. Annotated bibliographies and a name index.

S133. Grossberg, Lawrence, Cary Nelson, and Paula A. Treichler, *Cultural Studies.* New York: Routledge, 1992.

This important anthology of nearly eight hundred pages can best be navigated with the help of the "User's Guide" (pages 17-22), a topical table of contents. Rubrics include The History of Cultural Studies, Gender and Sexuality, Nationhood and National Identity, Colonialism and Postcolonialism, etc. Among the prominent essayists are Stuart Hall, Homi Bhabha, James Clifford, Cornell West, and bell hooks.

S134. Selden, Raman, and Peter Widdowson. *A Reader's Guide to Contemporary Literary Theory.* 3rd ed. Lexington: University of Kentucky Press, 1993.

A well-organized work with lucid presentations ranging from Eliot and Leavis to present-day Marxists, poststructuralists, postmodernists, postcolonialists, and feminists. Excellent selective bibliographies.

Approaches

S135. Belsey, Catherine. *Critical Practice.* London: Methuen, 1980. Bibliography, pp. 159-65.

S136. Harari, Josué V. *Textual Strategies: Perspectives in Post-Structuralist Criticism.* Ithaca: Cornell University Press, 1979. Bibliography, pp. 443-63.

S137. Hawkes, Terence. *Structuralism and Semiotics.* Berkeley: University of California Press, 1977. Bibliography, pp. 161-87.

S138. Jardine, Alice. *Gynesis: Configurations of Woman and Modernity.* Ithaca: Cornell University Press, 1985. Bibliography, pp. 265-77.

S139. Norris, Christopher. *Deconstruction: Theory and Practice.* Rev. ed. London: Routledge, 1991. Bibliography, pp. 159-92.

S140. Todorov, Tzvetan. *Theories of the Symbol.* Trans. Catherine Porter. Ithaca: Cornell University Press, 1982. Bibliography, pp. 201-12.

Journals

S141. *Critical Inquiry.* University of Chicago Press, 1974-. Quarterly.

S142. *Critical Quarterly.* Manchester: Manchester University Press, 1959-.

S143. *Critical Texts: A Review of Theory and Criticism.* Fayetteville, AR: Critical Texts, 1982-. Triannually.

S144. *Cultural Critique.* New York: Telos Press, 1985-. Triannually.

S145. *Cultural Studies.* London: Routledge, 1987-. Triannually.

S146. *Diacritics: A Review of Contemporary Criticism.* Ithaca: Department of Romance Studies, Cornell University, 1971-. Quarterly.

S147. *New Literary History: A Journal of Theory and Interpretation.* Baltimore: Johns Hopkins Universtiy Press, 1969-. Triannually.

S148. *Paragraph: The Journal of the Modern Critical Theory Group.* Oxford: Oxford University Press, 1983-. Biannually.

S149. *Poetics Today: A Central International Quarterly for Theory of Literature and Related Fields.* Tel Aviv: Porter Institute for Poetry and Poetics, 1979-. Quarterly.

S150. *Raritan: A Quarterly Review.* New Brunswick, NJ: Rutgers, 1981-. Quarterly.

S151. *Social Text: Theory, Culture, Ideology.* Madison, WI: Coda Press, 1979-. Quarterly.

S152. *Textual Practice.* London: Routledge, 1987-. Triannually.

RHETORIC, COMPOSITION STUDIES, TECHNICAL WRITING, AND WRITING ACROSS THE CURRICULUM

Abstracts

S153. *College Composition and Communication: The Journal of the Conference on College Composition and Communication.* Urbana, IL: National Council of Teachers of English, 1950-.

A quarterly concerned with composition research, pedagogy, and interdisciplinary relationships. As of 1975 (for 1973), during most years *CCC* has published an annual selective annotated bibliography of noteworthy books and articles in the theory and teaching of composition. The annotations are, in effect, abstracts. Subheadings: Bibliographies and Checklists; Theory and Research; Teacher Education, Administration and Social Roles; Curriculum; Textbooks and Instructional Materials; Testing, Measurement and Evaluation. The years 1984-85 were covered by the *Longman Bibliography of Composition and Rhetoric*, ed. Erika Lindemann (New York: Longman, 1987), thereafter by Southern Illinois UP.

S154. Linguistics and Language Behavior Abstracts. La Jolla, CA: Sociological Abstracts, 1967-. Formerly *Language and Language Behavior Abstracts.*

A quarterly, *LLBA* primarily abstracts linguistics and language journals, but includes journals of related fields such as rhetoric, semiotics, and education. Coverage is extensive since *LLBA* draws on some one thousand journals as well as other sources. At the back of each issue are author, source publication, and subject indexes. Book reviews are also listed. *LLBA* is available on-line.

S155. *Resources in Education.* Washington, DC: National Institute of Education, 1975-. Formerly *Research in Education.*

This monthly index with cumulations twice a year provides abstracts of ERIC (Educational Resources Information Center) documents—unpublished pedagogy-oriented research materials such as conference proceedings, speeches, essays, and bibliographies, many of which deal with composition. *RIE* abstracts allow you to determine which documents you might wish to examine. ERIC, a federally funded agency, makes all its holdings available on microfiche, and many libraries subscribe to the collection. The *Thesaurus of ERIC Descrip-tors* is the key to the *RIE* subject index of abstracts. Available on-line.

S156. *Technical Communication: Journal of the Society for Technical Communication.* Washington, D. C.: Society for Technical Communication, 1953-.

Since 1976 abstracts of important articles from some fifty journals have been listed in each quarterly issue under the rubric "Recent and Relevant."

Approaches

S157. Anderson, Paul V., R. John Brockmann, and Carolyn R. Miller, eds. *New Essays in Technical and Scientific Communication:*

Research, Theory, Practice. Baywood's Technical Communications Series 2. Farmingdale, NY: Baywood, 1983.

The twelve essays presented consider the problem of defining "technical" and "scientific" writing, set the two kinds of writing in a historical context, and suggest how technical writing might be redefined. The goal: to connect it with other forms of writing and make of it a creative and responsible endeavor. References to other relevant texts are included at the end of each essay.

S158. Donovan, Timothy R., and Ben W. McClelland, eds. *Eight Approaches to Teaching Composition.* Urbana, IL: National Council of Teachers of English, 1980-.

Attacks the strict "back to basics" approach to teaching writing. Eight alternative and diverse approaches are presented, selected for their accessibility, harmoniousness, and feasibility. Bibliography: pp. 151-58.

S159. Fearing, Bertie E., and W. Keats Sparrow. *Technical Writing: Theory and Practice.* New York: MLA, 1989.

Technical writers and instructors of the discipline discuss problems and issues. Thirteen essays in four parts: On the History and Theory of Technical Writing; On the Composing Process in Corporate Settings: From Industry to Academe; On the Process and Product of Technical Writing: Contemporary Perspectives; and On Teaching Technical Writing: Current and Recurrent Issues.

S160. Fulwiler, Toby, and Art Young, eds. *Language Connections: Writing and Reading Across the Curriculum.* Urbana, IL: National Council of Teachers of English, 1982.

This book is based on the assumption that writing, as a value-forming activity that not only conveys information but also provides students with a unique way of knowing, learning, and expressing their ideas, can play an important part in the curriculum of any discipline. The essays presented examine theoretical reasons and practical ideas for writing across the curriculum programs. Annotated bibliography: pp. 179-88. Also see these editors' recent collection *Programs that Work: Models and Methods for Writing Across the Curriculum* (Portsmouth, NH: Heinemann, 1990), in which professors at fourteen schools (e.g.,

Georgetown, UCLA, University of Vermont) discuss their WAC programs.

S161. Gere, Anne Ruggles, ed. *Into the Field: Sites of Composition Studies*. New York: MLA, 1993.

Essays by thirteen scholars on the interaction between composition and other disciplines and on the implications of postmodern notions of subjectivity for writing.

S162. Graves, Richard L., ed. *Rhetoric and Composition: A Sourcebook for Teachers and Writers*. 3rd ed. Portsmouth, NH: Boynton/Cook, 1990.

Thirty-one essays devoted to theory and practice: Stories from the Writing Classroom; Motivating Student Writing; Style; and New Perspectives, New Horizons (devoted largely to class and gender issues).

S163. Griffin, C. Williams, ed. *Teaching Writing in All Disciplines*. New Directions for Teaching and Learning Series. San Francisco: Jossey Bass, 1982.

A short volume divided into ten chapters that introduce writing across the curriculum. The first two chapters summarize relevant general composition theory. Several chapters discuss how teachers of mathematics, science, and business have used writing in their classrooms. The final chapters suggest how to start WAC programs. Most chapters conclude with lengthy reference lists.

S164. Horner, Winifred Bryan, ed. *The Present State of Scholarship in Historical and Contemporary Rhetoric*. Rev. ed. Columbia: University of Missouri Press, 1990.

Following a foreword by Walter Ong, S.J., six contributors discuss the rhetoric of various eras. Useful research projects are suggested. Bibliography.

S165. Kirsch, Gesa, and Patricia A. Sullivan, eds. *Methods and Methodology in Composition Research*. Carbondale: Southern Illinois University Press, 1992.

Virtually every approach to composition is mapped in this excellent survey of writing concepts and their actualization. Approaches include feminist, ethnographic, cognitive, historical, and others.

S166. Lindemann, Erika, and Gary Tate, eds. *An Introduction to Composition Studies*. New York: Oxford University Press, 1991.

Nine essays by major practitioners on such subjects as the relationships between rhetoric and composition and between concept and pedagogy. Problems encountered within the academic setting are discussed as well as methods and resources. Pp. 72-93 contain a valuable bibliography on resources and problems.

S167. McClelland, Ben W., and Timothy R. Donovan. *Perspectives on Research and Scholarship in Composition.* New York: MLA, 1985.

These essays present research in areas that continue to shape composition theory and pedagogy. Essay topics range widely, from "Toward a Theory of Composition" to "The Promise of Artificial Intelligence for Composition."

S168. McQuade, Donald, ed. *The Territory of Language: Linguistics, Stylistics, and the Teaching of Composition.* Carbondale: Southern Illinois University Press, 1986.

In this revised and enlarged edition of his 1979 compilation, McQuade draws together twenty-five essays, some new, some reprints, all intended to assist teachers in developing theoretically sound as well as feasible pedagogies. Includes a bibliographical essay on writing across the curriculum.

Bibliographies

S169. Bizzell, Patricia, and Herzberg, Bruce. *The Bedford Bibliography for Teachers of Writing*. 3rd ed. Boston: Bedford/St. Martin's, 1991.

This annotated and classified tool is the most recent book-length bibliography for composition. Categories include Periodicals; Bibliographies, Collections; The Rhetorical Tradition; Modern Rhetorical Theory; The Composing Process; Invention: Heuristics and Pre-Writing; Arrangement and Argument; Revision; Style; Basic Writing, Error Analysis, and Usage; and Teaching Composition. Includes CCCC and composition prize information.

CCCC Bibliography of Composition and Rhetoric (See S153.)

MLA International Bibliography. (See M7.)

S170. Moran, Michael G., and Debra Journet. *Research in Technical Communication: A Bibliographic Sourcebook.* Westport, CT: Greenwood, 1985.

Twenty-one contributors' essays introduce substantial bibliographies. Four sections: A Theoretic Examination of Technical Communication; Technical Communication and Rhetorical Concerns; Specific Types of Technical Communication (Projects; Technical Reports; Business Letters, Memoranda, and Resumés); Related Concerns and Specialized Forms of Technical Communication: Computing and the Future of Technical Communication; Oral Presentation and Presence in Business and Industry; Resources for Teaching Legal Writing; Writing for the Government. Appendices on textbooks, style manuals, and the profession.

S171. Moran, Michael G., and Ronald F. Lunsford. *Research in Composition and Rhetoric: A Bibliographic Sourcebook.* Westport, CT: Greenwood, 1984.

Considering composition and rhetoric from classical Greece to the present, the editors seek to validate and contextualize the field for composition teachers and researchers. Following Gary Tate's *Teaching Composition: Ten Bibliographical Essays* (Fort Worth: Texas Christian UP, 1976), they update and supplement his work. Part one connects current composition research with other fields such as linguistics, psychology, philosophy, and literature. Major issues such as grading take up another section. A third section is devoted to the "basics." Donald Stewart's appendix reviews textbooks. Index of authors at back. For recency, note that Andrea A. Lunsford provides useful bibliographies as "Suggestions for Further Reading" and "Works Cited and Recommended" appended to her survey essay "Rhetoric and Composition" in *Introduction to Scholarship in Modern Languages and Literatures*, 2nd ed., ed. Joseph Gibaldi (New York: MLA, 1992), 77-100, of which the last nine pages are bibliography.

S172. *Research in the Teaching of English.* Urbana, IL: National Council of Teachers of English, 1967-.

A quarterly publishing original research on the teaching and learning of language from preschool through adult levels. Aimed at a multidisciplinary audience. A brief abstract precedes each report. The "Annotated Bibliography of Research in the Teaching of English," a comprehensive listing, appears biannually.

S173. *Rhetoric Society Quarterly*. St. Cloud, MN: Rhetoric Society of America, 1968-. Formerly *Rhetoric Society Newsletter*.
A quarterly interested in rhetorical theory, criticism, history, pedagogy, research, and new developments. Publishes its "Current Bibliography" both quarterly and annually.

S174. Tate, Gary, ed. *Teaching Composition: Twelve Bibliographical Essays*. Rev. and enl. Fort Worth: Texas Christian University Press, 1987.
This revision of Tate's 1976 work (S171) surveys research on computers and composition, literacy issues, and literary aspects of non-narrative prose as well as the standard subjects.

S175. *Technical Communication Quarterly*. Morehead, KY: Association of Teachers of Techical Writing, 1974-. Formerly the *Technical Writing Teacher*.
A biannual journal publishing an annual international selective bibliography of books and articles on technical writing.

The Year's Work in English Studies. (See S42.)
See the rhetorical theory subdivision in the chapter on literary theory (1981-). Index to critics and to authors and subjects treated at back.

Handbooks and Guides

S176. Houp, Kenneth W., and Thomas E. Pearsall. *Reporting Technical Information*. 8th ed. Boston: Allyn and Bacon, 1995.
A detailed explanation of general report preparation and of specific kinds of writing: proposals, progress reports, feasibility reports, correspondence, etc. Extensive diagrams and samples.

S177. Woodson, Linda. *A Handbook of Modern Rhetorical Terms.* Urbana, IL: National Council of Teachers of English, 1979.

Woodson's purpose is to "bring together in one place the myriad of words that have been added to rhetoric and composition in this century" (Preface). Each term is not only defined but also explained by example with references to specific books or articles in which the term has been used. Following the alphabetically arranged *Handbook* proper, an appendix lists the words under such headings as "Classifications of Discourse" and "General Rhetorical Terms." Index of authors cited.

Journals

College Composition and Communication: The Journal of the Conference on College Composition and Communication. (See S153.)

S178. *College English.* Urbana, IL: National Council of Teachers of English, 1939-. Monthly, September through April.

S179. *Composition Studies.* Fort Worth: Texas Christian University, 1972-. Triannually. Formerly *Freshman English News.*

Research in the Teaching of English. (See S172.)

S180. *Rhetorica: A Journal of the History of Rhetoric.* Berkeley: University of California Press, 1983-. Quarterly.

S181. *Rhetoric Review: A Journal of Rhetoric and Composition.* University of Arizona, 1982-. Biannually.

Rhetoric Society Quarterly. (See S173.)

Technical Communication Quarterly (See S175.)

INDEX

ABOUT THE AUTHOR

Dorothea Kehler is a professor of English at San Diego State University. Previous editions of her *Problems in Literary Research* appeared in 1975, 1981, and 1987. She is co-editor with Susan Baker of *In Another Country: Feminist Perspectives on Renaissance Drama* (Metuchen, NJ: Scarecrow, 1991). Professor Kehler has published essays on Shakespeare in *Shakespeare Quarterly*, *Shakespeare Jahrbuch*, *Renaissance Papers*, and various other scholarly journals. She is currently editing the volume on *A Midsummer Night's Dream* for Garland Publishing's Shakespearean Criticism series.